Finding Out About
The Russians

Finding God Among The Russians

Jim Forest

LAMP

Marshall Morgan and Scott
Lamp Press
34 – 42 Cleveland Street, London W1P 5FB

First published in 1989 by Marshall Morgan and Scott Publications Ltd
Part of the Marshall Pickering Holdings Group

British Library CIP Data

Forest, Jim
  Finding God among the Russians. — 2nd ed
  1. Soviet Union. Russkaia pravoslavnaia
  tserkov
  I. Title
  281.9'47

  ISBN: 0 551 01630 2

Text set in Baskerville by Brian Robinson, Buckingham
Printed and bound in Great Britain by
Cox & Wyman Ltd, Reading

FINDING GOD AMONG THE RUSSIANS

Jim Forest

To my Mother, Marguerite Hendrickson Forest

"Lord, how good everything is . . .
You only have to look around you!"

— Maxim Gorky's grandmother, in his book
My Childhood

Contents

PREFACE

A decade before his death, Thomas Merton noted in his journal the realization that reconciliation is not simply a formal coming together of people who have been divided. The healing of broken relationships is rooted in our spiritual lives:

> If I can unite *in myself* the thought and devotion of Eastern and Western Christendom, the Greek and the Latin Fathers, the Russians and the Spanish mystics, I can prepare in myself the reunion of divided Christians. From that secret and unspoken unity in myself can eventually come a visible and manifest unity of all Christians. If we want to bring together what is divided, we cannot do so by imposing one division upon the other. If we do this, the union is not Christian. It is political and doomed to further conflict. We must contain all the divided worlds in ourselves and transcend them in Christ.[1]

One of the books that stirred Merton's fascination with the Russian mystics was Boris Pasternak's novel, *Doctor Zhivago*. He was impressed by the "striking and genuinely Christian elements in the outlook of Pasternak, in the philosophy that underlies his writing."[2] In 1958, despite the formidable barrier between the United States and the Soviet Union, Merton entered into correspondence with Pasternak. He began reading books on Russian Orthodox theology and spirituality and even started studying the Russian language, events which must have been startling within a community of American Trappist monks. Undoubtedly this development in Merton's life was a significant factor in the subsequent

1. Thomas Merton, *Conjectures of a Guilty Bystander* (New York: Doubleday & Co., 1966), p. 12.
2. "The Pasternak Affair," in *Disputed Questions* (New York: Farrar, Straus and Cudahy, 1960); the essay is also included in *The Literary Essays of Thomas Merton* (New York: New Directions, 1981).

writing he did on issues of peace and nonviolence.[3]

I recall the impact Pasternak's novel had on me in 1958. I was a high school student in Hollywood, California, altogether uninterested in Christianity in Russia or anywhere else, as I considered myself an agnostic. Yet, because of *Dr. Zhivago*, Russia was no longer merely a cage of forbidding Cold War imagery.

A few years later, having found my way to religious belief, I joined the Catholic Worker community in New York City. While there, I came to know the community's founder, Dorothy Day, and the special devotion she had to Russian writers, Dostoyevsky most of all, but many others, including Gorky, Tolstoy, Chekhov and Solzhenitsyn.[4] This was matched by her love of the Russian Orthodox Church. Several times she took me with her to attend the Orthodox Liturgy sung in Slavonic.

One evening Dorothy brought me to a Manhattan apartment for a meeting of the Third Hour, a Christian ecumenical group founded by a Russian émigrée scholar, Helene Iswolsky.[5]

The conversation was about Russian Orthodox spirituality — *dukhovnost* — a word far richer in meaning than its English counterpart, suggesting not only a personal relationship between the praying person and God but moral capacity, social responsibility, courage, wisdom, mercy, a readiness to forgive, a way of life centred on love. Much of the discussion flew over my head. I was more attentive to the remarkable face of W.H. Auden, a member of the Third Hour

3. For details of the Merton-Pasternak correspondence, see Michael Mott, *The Seven Mountains of Thomas Merton* (Boston: Houghton Mifflin Co., 1984), pp. 322-25. Also note Jim Forest, *Thomas Merton's Struggle with Peacemaking* (Erie, PA: Benet Press, n.d.) and *Thomas Merton: A Pictorial Biography* (Mahwah, NJ: Paulist Press, 1980); Thomas Merton, *The Nonviolent Alternative* (New York: Farrar, Straus & Giroux, 1971), *Gandhi on Nonviolence* (New York: New Directions, 1965), and *Faith and Violence* (Notre Dame, IN: University of Notre Dame Press, 1968).

4. Jim Forest, *Love Is the Measure: A Biography of Dorothy Day* (Mahwah, NJ: Paulist Press, and Basingstoke, England: Marshall Pickering, 1986); note especially reference to Dostoyevsky and to her travels in Russia, pp. 175-77.

5. Helene Iswolsky, *No Time to Grieve: An Autobiography* (Philadelphia: Winchell Co., 1985) and *Christ in Russia* (Milwaukee: Bruce Publishing Co., 1960).

group. But I recall talk about the "holy fools" who wandered Russia in continuous pilgrimage, reciting with every breath and step the silent prayer, "Lord Jesus Christ, Son of the living God, have mercy on me, a sinner." From that evening this prayer became part of my own spiritual life.

In 1969-70, having been part of a Catholic group of war resisters who burned draft records to protest the Vietnam war, I spent a year in prison. It was only then that I was at last un-busy enough to read the Russian writers Dorothy had so often recommended. I hadn't intended to spend so much of that year with Russian authors, but each book led me to another. The three that brought Russia most alive for me were Gorky's autobiographical books, *My Childhood*, *My Apprenticeship*, and *My Universities*. It is only a slight exaggeration to say that his grandmother became my grandmother. I am not sure whether it is Gorky or myself remembering her passionate prayers before the icons in the corner of her room.[6] Ever since prison, Gorky's grandmother has been part of my life. As much as Dorothy Day, she opened the door to "Holy Mother Russia."

My profession is journalism. Much of my adult life has been spent editing peace movement publications. One might think such work would have opened many East-West doors. Ironically, however, for many years the peace movement in the United States was notable for its avoidance of contact with the Soviet Union. Perhaps because we were so routinely accused of being "tools of the Kremlin," peace activists tended to steer clear of Russia and rarely knew more about it than anyone else. To utter a friendly word about the Soviet Union was to be convicted of everything the *Reader's Digest* had ever said about KGB direction of peace groups in the west.

In the spring of 1982, after five years living in Europe while serving as General Secretary of the International Fellowship of Reconciliation (IFOR), I was on a speaking trip that took me to twenty cities in nearly every part of America. At the time the Nuclear Freeze movement was gathering strength. It seemed to me, however, that despite the millions of people

6. Maxim Gorky, *My Childhood* (New York: Penguin Books, 1966), pp. 60-74.

supporting the Freeze, the prospects for quick changes in the relationship between the US and USSR were slight. The Freeze, like so many other peace campaigns, was built mainly on fear of nuclear weapons. Practically nothing was being done to respond to relationship issues or the fear of the Soviet Union that underlies public acceptance of the arms race.[7] All that was needed was one nasty incident to burst the balloon, and that came when a Soviet pilot shot down a Korean passenger plane flying across Soviet air space. The image of the west facing a barbaric and ruthless enemy was instantly revived and the Freeze movement lost its momentum. (Fortunately in more recent years both Churches and peace organizations have developed major programmes of contact and dialogue linking American and Soviet citizens.)[8]

At the end of the speaking trip, while in Cambridge, Massachusetts, Robert Ellsberg took me to see *Moscow Doesn't Believe in Tears*. I was reluctant to go, assuming it would be a propaganda exercise, but Robert said that the film had been awarded an Oscar and, more to the point, was one of the funniest movies he had seen in months. He was eager to see it a second time, so we ate a Mexican meal and went to the movies.

Moscow Doesn't Believe in Tears is about economic and social classes in the "classless" society. Centring on three women who arrive in Moscow in 1960, the film follows their struggles to build careers and families. Despite differences in temperament and ambition, they create an enduring friendship. Midway the film jumps to the 1970s, so that we see what has happened to them after the passage of fifteen years. The stories told are comical, tragic, convincing and socially revealing. Muscovites became quite three-dimensional and not simply cardboard figures living in the grey world of communism.

7. In February 1987, a public opinion poll in the United States indicated that two-thirds of the American people believed that the Soviet Union would like to invade and occupy the United States and that 72 per cent preferred all-out nuclear war to life under communist rule. See John M. Swomley, "Myths That Separate Us," *Fellowship* 53 (December 1987) pp. 5-6.

8. These include the Fellowship of Reconciliation, which runs a US-USSR Reconciliation Programme through which information is available on a wide variety of opportunities for contact and education. FOR, Box 271, Nyack, NY 10960.

Coupled with the speaking trip, the film brought home to me the startling truth that most of us in the peace movement knew far more about weapons than the people at whom the weapons were aimed. I began to look for an opportunity to travel in the Soviet Union.

At the time it wasn't easy to find an opening. The Soviet Union was at war in Afghanistan, an event sharply condemned by the movement I was working for. A seminar we had arranged in Moscow was abruptly cancelled on the Soviet side. An editor of *Izvestia* with whom I had breakfast in Amsterdam candidly explained that there was anxiety in the Kremlin that pacifists from the west might unveil protest signs in Red Square. "We are not all so stupid, but neither are we all so smart," he said. "Try again. Next time you may get a smarter bureaucrat."

In the fall of 1983, Lubomir Mirejovsky, a Czech pastor, who is General Secretary of the Christian Peace Conference (CPC), suggested that representatives of our two movements meet for a dialogue on the subject of "Violence, Nonviolence and Liberation." We agreed to the proposal. Metropolitan Fileret of Minsk, head of the External Church Affairs Department of the Russian Orthodox Church and Chairman of the CPC's Continuation Committee, invited us to have the meeting at his office in Moscow.

The days in Moscow that October went quickly. Much of our time was taken up by meetings, which turned out to be quite lively, with a depth and candour that I hadn't anticipated. Our time for tourist activity, unfortunately, was minimal. We had a brief visit to the Kremlin. One night we were at the ballet, the next at the circus. Attempting to keep up with the Russians as toast after toast was proposed, I managed to get embarrassingly wobbly at the one meal we ate in a private home.

The most rewarding experiences of that first trip were on the first and last nights. The first night, encouraged by a clear sky and full moon, I walked with a British colleague to the Kremlin and Red Square. And on the last night I set off entirely by myself, an experience recorded in the following diary entry:

Skipping supper, I had time to explore the Metro, Moscow's subway system. Dimitri, a translator assisting our meeting, gave me a map, marking stations he especially recommended. I walked to the Kievskaya station, was caught up in the rush-hour current, put a five-kopek coin in the turnstile, went down the crowded escalator. For the first time in my life I was on my own among Russian people.

My project was to explore half-a-dozen stations but it wasn't always easy to easy to know where I was. My map was in English, the signs in Russian. This proved a fast way to learn basics of the Cyrillic alphabet.

The stations are everything they are said to be: no two alike, immaculate, free of graffiti. Some have an almost Moorish simplicity, some resemble baroque churches. The decoration includes mosaics, stained glass and sculpture. In one station, crystal chandeliers run the length of the central corridor between platforms and above the train tracks as well. Each station is a work of art.

But what stirred me most was simply to be in the thick of Russian people. While some wore the military uniforms, the centre piece of western imagery of the USSR, most people were in clothing that wouldn't attract special notice in London or New York — nothing fancy, but nothing threadbare either. The differences were less striking than the similarities. As for the faces, I could have found all of them, and the moods they registered, in any bus or subway in North America or West Europe.

As it was early in the evening when I started out, the passengers included children. One round-faced child stared at me — perhaps because of my beard — with an expression divided between shyness and curiosity. Sitting on her father's lap, gripping his hand, her head pressed against his chest, she looked like my seven-year-old Wendy.

In New York, where subways are an ordeal, I was always grateful whenever a couple in love came into the car. They changed the atmosphere in a remarkable way, dissolving the tension and anxiety. I felt blessed by them and felt others did too. The fact that couples of the same sort ride the Moscow Metro somehow surprised me. It was a revelation of how dehumanized our perceptions have become after so many years of readiness for war. But of course people fall in love in the Soviet Union as passionately as they do anywhere in the world. In one crowded

Metro car, I happened to be jammed against a young couple whose heads were gently inclined toward each other so that their noses touched. They were oblivious to everyone around them.

No less important than people-watching was having to ask for help in stations where Metro lines intersect. Each time I found someone who not only would point the way but take me to the right platform. It was encouraging to discover how much could be done despite language barriers.

That first trip in the USSR was something like riding through a museum of fine arts on a bicycle. I saw wonderful things, but too fast to take them in and with far too little understanding of Russian and Soviet history to make much sense of even those things which weren't a blur. But the trip was enough for me to know that I wanted to come back, see things more slowly, and talk with Russians. I had a particular sense of connection with the Russian Orthodox Church and longed to have the chance to meet believers informally and face to face.

Back in Holland, I wrote to Archbishop (now Metropolitan) Pitirim, head of the Publishing Department of the Moscow Patriarchate, asking if I might have the cooperation of his department in writing a book about Russian Orthodoxy. It would not be, I wrote to him, an academic work. Others had done such books and in any event I was not qualified. But I had spent much of my adult life doing interviews for peace and church magazines, worked for various newspapers and press services, had written two biographies and many essays. I felt I could write a book about Russian believers, if the church could provide a translator and help me visit centres of Orthodoxy — churches, seminaries, and monasteries.

While it took a long time to make all the arrangements, the letter eventually received a positive response.

In discussing this book with friends, the question was sometimes asked: Why only the Russian Orthodox Church? Why not other churches and religious groups in the Soviet Union? My answer is that I have found myself particularly at home in Russian Orthodox churches. But one can add, however, that, with an estimated fifty-million members, the

Russian Orthodox Church is the largest religious body in the Soviet Union and the most deeply rooted institution of Russian culture. At the same time, Orthodoxy is quite foreign to western Christians who often find its ornate ritual and imagery, not to mention its patriarchal structure, positively revolting. If there is ever to be a drawing together of Christians across their many divisions, we need to have a much deeper understanding of Orthodoxy. (Even so, I hope to write a book about other religious communities in the USSR.)

The text that follows is based on letters I wrote to my wife, Nancy, in the course of my travels in the USSR. The letters form a daybook. The last section of the book owes much to the journal Nancy kept while we were travelling together last summer. While I considered organizing the text thematically rather than as a journal, to do so would have obliterated the gradual process of discovery. Thus certain topics like worship and icons are touched on repeatedly. These are at the heart of the Orthodox spiritual life and continue to open in new and often surprising ways for me.

Some readers will miss attention in these pages to the "suffering Church." Especially in the '20s and '30s, the Church produced many martyrs. Thousands of churches were closed. Many bishops, priests, nuns and lay believers were imprisoned or executed. While Stalin's policy changed in a more positive direction following Hitler's attack on the USSR, even to the present day believers have often been penalized for their faith, especially if they expressed resistance. Also Bibles and prayer books are produced in far smaller quantities than are needed. Such aspects of Soviet life, however, have been the subject of many books and thousands of press articles. My concern here is to show what is so often ignored, the vitality and hospitality of the Church despite its innumerable sorrows and difficulties.

The work on this book has had a quite unexpected impact on my spiritual and family life. Soon after my first trip to Moscow, Nancy started cooking occasional Russian meals. More important, each night we began to pray before Russian icons, standing up as Russians do and often using prayers the Orthodox liturgy. Perhaps I was more surprised than any of my friends when I finally took the step of joining the Russian Orthodox Church, being received a week ago, Palm Sunday, by Fr. Alexis Voogd and the congregation of the Church of St. Nicholas of Myra in Amsterdam. Nancy looks forward to taking the same step on Pentecost.

Jim Forest
Second Day of Easter, 1988
Alkmaar, Holland

ACKNOWLEDGEMENTS

First of all, within the Russian Orthodox Church, I am indebted to Metropolitan Pitirim of Volokolamsk, head of the Publishing Department, and his assistant Tatiana Volgina; and to Metropolitan Fileret of Minsk, head of the Department of External Church Affairs, and to Georgi Derevianchenko, assistant to the chairman of that department. I also owe special thanks to Vasili Maknev, Fr. Boris Udovenko, Archdeacon Vladimir Nazarkin, Nina Babrova, Fr. Georgi Goncharov, Vladimir and Ludmilla Tyschuk, and Tatiana Tchernikova.

My thanks also go to Diana Francis, President of the International Fellowship of Reconciliation, and other members of the IFOR Steering Committee, who allowed me time to travel in the USSR. Without their encouragement and support, this book would have been impossible.

The friendship and help of Gene Knudsen-Hoffman have been essential.

Among others outside the USSR who have helped in a variety of ways, I especially must mention Joseph Peacock, Fr. Alexis Voogd, Rev. Lubomir Mirejovsky, Richard Deats, Virginia Baron, W.H. Ferry, Sr. Mary Evelyn Jegen, Françoise Pottier, Prof. Robert Tusler, Peggy Attlee, Stephen Tunnicliffe, Prof. Dr. Hannes de Graaf, Lee Weingarten, Cheryl Cayford and the staff of the bookshop of the Russian Orthodox Cathedral at Ennismore Gardens in London.

The saying is that there are no good authors, only good editors. In my case these are Michael Leach of Crossroad/Continuum in New York and, at Marshall Pickering in England, Debbie Thorpe.

Finally, my gratitude goes to my wife, Nancy. These pages

reflect a pilgrimage we have been making together. The text was first of all a thick sheaf of letters to her. She has since then helped me in the work of revision. Her own diary for the Russian trip we took together last summer, during which I only kept notes, was the starting point of the final section of this book.

OCTOBER 1984

In the fall of 1984 I received a telex from Archbishop Pitirim of Volokolamsk, head of the Publishing Department of the Moscow Patriarchate, inviting me to Moscow to discuss my proposal to write a book about the Russian Orthodox Church. The visit was extended a further week in order to take part in a meeting of representatives of the International Fellowship of Reconciliation and the Soviet Peace Committee.

Moscow, October 19, 1984:

The afternoon flight of KLM from Amsterdam to Moscow stops briefly in Warsaw. Coming down I had a good look at farms in the surrounding region. The fields are often thin strips, making a patchwork quilt that has no coherent pattern, neighbours linked by dirt roads. Not much traffic.

The cloud cover over western Russia prevented even a glimpse of the land, but we had an above-the-clouds view of a sunset that turned all the western sky blood-red.

In the Moscow airport, the person checking my bags took a great interest in a book of wood engravings by Fritz Eichenberg, many of which have a religious theme. Finally he summoned his superior. The scrutiny they gave to these pages will reassure Fritz that art continues to be a high-risk vocation. I think what finally got me through without loss of any books or papers was the indignant fuss I made.

In the waiting area beyond customs, Tatiana Tchernikova introduced herself. A slim woman with auburn hair, she is a member of the staff of the Department for External Church Affairs of the Russian Orthodox Church. A battered car and friendly driver were waiting in the parking lot. On our way into central Moscow, I mentioned Fred Mayer's remarkable photos in *The Orthodox Church in Russia*.[1] It turns out Tanya, as she suggests I call her, travelled with Mayer when he was taking the photos.

We went to the Ukraina Hotel, one of Moscow's monumental heaps of stone left from the Stalin years, a kind of granite wedding cake. It stands on the bank of the Moskva River a few miles west of Red Square. After getting me

1. Archbishop Pitirim of Volokolamsk, ed., *The Orthodox Church in Russia,* with photographs by Fred Mayer (New York: Vendome Press, and London: Thames & Hudson, 1982).

registered, Tanya was off, promising to return for breakfast. Unable to sleep, I decided to walk to the Kremlin. This took me down Kalinin Prospekt past a parade of sleek modern buildings. Getting closer to the Kremlin (the Russian word for fortress), older buildings began to appear, including a former church, its onion domes intact but the crosses lopped off. Now an exhibition hall, it must have been a beautiful church in its day.

A year ago I first walked this avenue. It was a later hour, when there was hardly a soul to be seen and practically no traffic. On the way back on that first walk, it was past midnight, which meant that I had this wide thoroughfare entirely to myself. I remember wondering, "Is someone watching me? Can a lone American wander around Moscow without KGB accompaniment?" I occasionally looked behind me but there was no one in sight. Once in my hotel room, I wondered if there was a microphone hidden in the wall or behind a painting.

What I discovered that first night in Moscow last year was that my head was an attic stuffed with vivid Cold War imagery. The attic is by no means empty a year later, but this time there were fewer glances backward.

Red Square was glistening beautifully in the rain. St. Basil's Cathedral stood in a flood of light at the far end of the vast space, Lenin's tomb midway down the Kremlin wall on the right, the GUM department store on the left, the red-brick History Museum in back of me. The cobblestone surface is dark as sea water at night but, wet, is full of light. This is really one of the most impressive public squares in the world. Judging from old paintings and photos, it has changed surprisingly little under revolutionary auspices. St. Basil's Cathedral is Red Square's exclamation point. Lenin's Tomb is austere and understated, not in competition with St. Basil's. How funny that a church has become *the* symbol of a "godless" state.

October 20:

Tanya, freed from her desk for most of my stay, asked what I would especially like to do and see in Moscow. We spoke about various church services. There is a monastery near her office where there are services morning and evening. There is also the Tretyakov Gallery, which I have long been hoping to see. I would love to have an unhurried look at the churches inside the Kremlin which I hurried through during a meeting intermission last year.

We started with the Kremlin cathedrals.

Russian churches are so different in spirit than churches in western Europe. They seem playful, like water colours for a child's book. What could be more fanciful than a crop of upside-down onions growing into the sky? Some of the cupolas are shining gold, some dull green, others dark blue with gold stars. Most amazing are the multi-coloured cupolas of St. Basil's.

"The architects tried to suggest candle flames by the cupola shape," said Tanya, "but people always think of onions." She reminded me of the story Dostoyevsky tells in *The Brothers Karamazov* of a self-centered woman almost saved from hell by an onion. " 'But she wasn't entirely selfish,' an angel reminded God. 'Remember, she once gave an onion to a hungry beggar.' 'Yes, that's true,' God said. 'I bless you to use that onion to lift her out of hell.' The angel took the onion and found the stingy woman. She grabbed hold of the onion and was being lifted up, but those standing near her wanted to come with her and hung on to her legs. The woman wanted heaven only for herself, so she kicked the others away. 'Just me,' she screamed, 'just me!' As she said these words her hands slipped from the onion and she fell back into hell."

For many years my greatest love among churches was

4

Chartres, the thirteenth-century gothic cathedral in the countryside southwest of Paris. It is what a monk I know calls a "thin place." For all its stone, Chartres has a kind of transparency. Its wordless celebration of the existence of God is a never-ending wonder. It isn't simply the architecture or the windows or the carving. The building seems soaked with the confessions, the prayers, the hopes and loves of all those it has drawn into itself since its walls began to rise.

More recently, especially in these years since moving to Europe, romanesque churches centuries older than Chartres have endeared themselves to me. While not nearly so majestic and mysterious as the great gothic churches, they imply a more maternal God, a God of gentle touches, a God who can be relied on completely, a God as solid as a Roman arch.

There is in Russian churches neither the heaven-climbing ambition of gothic architecture nor the solemnization of gravity offered by romanesque tradition. These Russian churches are an invitation – not only to believe and to pray but to experience the mystical life.

Among the four Kremlin churches that we visited, the one that most impressed me today was the Cathedral of the Archangel Michael. Many of the czars are buried here, including Ivan the Terrible. It is a church that links itself to the Last Judgment, as one sees from the fresco over the door. Inside, everything is icons but the floor. There is very little gold, which is surprising when you think how much gold and silver ended up in Russian churches. The colours are subdued earth shades: dark green, an orange like the dried peel of a tangerine, a creamy ivory white. I noticed scenes of Creation, Eden, the Fall, and the Resurrection of the Dead. Overhead was a huge icon of Christ enthroned, orange-red triangles and half circles surrounding him, a blast of energy and yet utter calm, motion and perfect stillness.

The iconostasis in a Russian Church is an iconed wall with several doors. The Royal Doors are in the centre and beyond them the altar. I used to think of the iconostasis as an unfortunate border drawn between priests and lay people but now I realize it is the place in the church for the main icons, which, if you understand icons as an encouragement to pray, may be the best place to put them.

The artists who made icons were trying to paint openings into eternity. Even in museum churches, they still inspire prayer, as I could see in some of the faces of visitors I saw today. One young woman stood before an icon of Mary and Jesus and crossed herself. On the other hand, there are those quite disconnected from icons, who see in them simply works of historic significance, primitive steps along the path to modern painting. I noticed one visitor, using the glass over an icon as a mirror, tidying her hair.

In the evening, Tanya brought me to a yellow-brick building housing the Publishing Department of the Moscow Patriarchate. One flight up is the office of Archbishop Pitirim, a large room with a cluttered desk at one end and a tidy reception area at the other, a long conference table in the middle, windows filling one wall, books and icons on the facing wall.

Archbishop Pitirim has a face as warm as a fireplace. He has a long grey beard and long hair on his head: the traditional Orthodox acceptance of hair as a gift from God. His eyebrows are thick and dark, almost black. He has large, welcoming eyes, the eyes of a story teller.

"We Christians have the obligation to overcome, even liquidate, the image of the enemy," he said. "The only real enemies we have are sin and death. As Billy Graham said when he was in Moscow, all people in the world together face a common enemy, not each other but war itself. Such an enemy as war comes from our enemy-images. The subject of enemies must be considered theologically rather than politically."

In addition to his responsibility for the Church's publishing work, Archbishop Pitirim teaches a course on the New Testament at the Moscow Theological Academy. We spoke about the church at the time when the New Testament was written: "The early Christians did not search for the enemy in others," he said, "but in themselves. Inspired by the scriptures, they patiently turned to the transformation of themselves. In this way they transformed their world. This is the kind of moral development needed today if we are to overcome enmity. We must begin with the transformation of ourselves rather than someone else. And we must search for what is good in whoever is called 'an enemy.' ''

On the way back to the hotel, travelling alone, I had a nice encounter with strangers in the Metro. Two students helped me find the right platform, then asked me if I like the poetry of Robert Burns. We ended up singing ''Auld Lang Syne.''

October 21:

After breakfast Tanya took me to the Tretyakov Gallery. I had never heard of it until my first visit to Moscow and then only just before leaving.

Several of the most sublime icons in the world are in the Tretyakov, including Our Lady of Vladimir, Rublev's Holy Trinity, Rublev's icon of the Saviour, and a crucifixion by Dionysius.

Icons such as Our Lady of Vladimir are distinguished from other icon types by a Russian word meaning "tender loving." This is because Jesus and Mary aren't presented in stiff royal poses but with their faces pressed gently together. The icon of Our Lady of Vladimir has been in Russia since 1155, when it was brought from Constantinople to Kiev and then to Suzdal. In 1161 it was taken to Vladimir, after which its name is taken. "Chronicles record every time it was moved from one place to another," writes Vladimir Lossky, "and explain by its influence every important event in Russian history. . . [it] is venerated as the greatest holy treasure of the nation."[2]

Though judged by art historians as having been painted in Constantinople in the eleventh or twelfth century, the icon is regarded by many Orthodox believers as the work of the author of the third Gospel, St. Luke. The tradition is understandable. One can easily imagine this *is* Mary. She gazes out from the battered surface of the icon with deep love and concern, while her head is tilted toward the child in her arms. It is a painting of every mother and child, and yet unmistakably this is the Mother of God, and in her arms is the Lord of Life. The anxiety in Mary's face anticipates the crucifixion. It also suggests every parent's apprehension for

2. Leonid Ouspensky and Vladimir Lossky, *The Meaning of Icons* (Crestwood, NY: St. Vladimir's Seminary Press, 1982), p. 96.

their children's lives. But the Christ child's face is free of worry. One of his hands is around her neck, the other resting just beneath her shoulder. In expression and touch he offers silent, motionless reassurance.

Andrei Rublev painted the Holy Trinity icon in the mid-1420s. It was intended as the principal icon of the Holy Trinity Lavra, to be placed to the right of the Doors in the iconostasis of the Holy Trinity Cathedral. Three golden-winged figures sit on gold thrones around a table, the altar. At the centre of the altar is a gold chalice holding a burnt offering. In the background are a house, a tree and a mountain. The image is familiar to me. Henri Nouwen gave us an excellent reproduction of it as a wedding gift and it hangs over the fireplace in our living room. I was unprepared, however, at how much depth and light there is in the actual icon, how transparent it is, and how big, at least a yard wide.

The angelic figures are the three strangers that appeared to Abraham at Mamre: "And the Lord appeared to him by the oaks of Mamre, as he sat at the door of his tent in the heat of the day."[3] In Genesis the three are recognized as Lord and described both in the singular and plural. Sarah made bread for them while Abraham had a calf slaughtered for their meal. She laughed at their assurance that she would have a child: "After I have waxed old, shall I have pleasure?"[4] In the Rublev icon, neither Abraham nor Sarah are visible. Rublev's attention is not on the details of the story but only on the three strangers, in whom Orthodox believers recognize the Trinity.

The outer edge of the three figures forms a perfect circle. Within the circle a triangle is suggested. But neither shape is stressed. What you see first are three young faces inclined toward each other. The faces are not patriarchal. Rather they look like three identical sisters. The three are so engaged with each other that there is an overwhelming oneness in them. There is no argument, there is nothing aggressive. No one dominates. They are united in silent, intimate dialogue. One

3. Genesis 18:1. All biblical quotations taken from the Revised Standard Version.
4. Genesis 18:12.

9

is drawn into their silence and into the love it contains. There are no words for this. You are invited to be present in their love, to be forgiven and healed in this love, to be saved in this love.

At the centre of their love is sacrifice: the burnt offering in the chalice. The tree in the background suggests the wood on which Christ was crucified. The barren mountain is a reminder both of the Mount of Temptation and the Mount of Transfiguration. The house, as Henri Nouwen has written, is "the house of mercy, the house of perfect love, the house of God."[5] The door is open. All can enter. Everyone is invited.

In Rublev's icon called the Saviour of Zvenigorod, also known as "the Peacemaker", one is face to face with Jesus, as if a door had been opened and he was suddenly standing there. His eyes are kind but romanticize nothing. His face seems to contain the whole gospel. Looking at it one can experience both judgment and forgiveness, authority and mercy. No single word and quality of Jesus dominates. Such stillness! It is a miracle that this image has survived. A year after the Revolution of 1917, it was found in a barn.

The Dionysius icon of the crucifixion dates from 1500 and probably is connected to the biblical verse, "Woman, behold, your son!"[6] Four women, with Mary in the centre, stand to one side, on the other the disciple John, to whom Jesus commended his mother, and a soldier. In the air around Christ are angels. It isn't a bloody scene. Christ seems weightless, calm and gentle. His inclined face resembles the faces in Rublev's Holy Trinity icon. Jesus' gaze is toward his mother. Despite the distance, the faces of Jesus and Mary seem to touch as they do in the icon of Our Lady of Vladimir. Even while dying, Jesus offers his mother reassurance. The heads of Jesus, Mary and John are the corners of a triangle, another suggestion of the Trinity.

After a long stay with the icons, we concentrated on work

5. Henri Nouwen, *Behold the Beauty of the Lord: Praying with Icons* (Notre Dame, IN: Ave Maria Press, 1987), pp. 19-27.
6. John 19:26.

10

by the Itinerants, a school of Russian artists active in the late 1800s and early 1900s. Their style is quite realistic and direct. The canvases say a great deal about what brought on the Revolution. Often we see how desperate life was for the poor a hundred years ago. There are also damning glimpses of the rich. Occasionally the artists concentrate on the comfort and self-absorbtion of clerics, yet many of these artists are trying to affirm the gospels. In these cases their work is sometimes a kind of modern iconography.

In Nicholas Ghe's painting (done in 1890) of Christ before Pilate, Pilate is asking, "What is truth?" Christ stands before Pilate wearing the dark red robe the soldiers put on him as a crude joke. His hands are bound behind him. Still and silent as an icon, he stands gazing at Pilate. Young, fearless, with dishevelled hair, he looks like a revolutionary. The face has much in common with icons of Christ Pantocratur: Jesus shown as the Lord and Judge of Life.

In the same room is Ghe's "Golgotha," painted in 1893. An accusing arm points at Christ from the left. Perhaps it is a soldier ordering Jesus to take off his robe. The face of Christ is full of anguish and grief. He looks very Jewish. His eyes are closed, his hands at the sides of his face, the fingers pulling back the skin of his forehead. At his side are the two other condemned men, one of whom has an expression of murderous rage, while the other has a sorrowful calm about him.

I left the Tretyakov Gallery aware that it is one of Moscow's living churches.

In the afternoon I had a daytime look at Red Square. There were many thousands there but the space is so vast that it didn't seem crowded. The vivid colours of the cupolas of St. Basil's kept anchoring my eyes. The flow of newly married couples to Lenin's Tomb (they are exempted from having to wait in line) is nearly constant on Saturdays. Afterward the couples leave flowers at the eternal flame for the unknown soldier on the Kremlin's north wall.

"The wedding gowns are all handmade," Tanya said, "often the work of the brides or their mothers, otherwise the

11

work of friends.'' I watched one couple walking dreamily together, oblivious to the parade of relatives and friends behind them.

Nearly everyone on the Square is Russian or at least Russian speaking, though often one hears a quite unfamiliar language or sees strikingly Asiatic faces. Many people and groups pose for pictures with St. Basil's behind them. Near Lenin's tomb, people are hushed, the atmosphere church-like. But on the rest of the square it is like a country fair: laughter, ice cream, children riding on the shoulders of their fathers.

Sunday, October 22:

The high point of the day may well be the high point of all these days in Russia: simply being present for the Liturgy this morning in the Epiphany Cathedral.

Epiphany Cathedral isn't an old church. The place is drenched in gold, as if King Midas went on a rampage and happened to be here when it happened. The icons, of the western-influenced style of the eighteenth and nineteenth centuries, are not to my taste. And yet being in this throng of worshippers was a more exciting experience than I have had in far more beautiful churches. In fact the place became beautiful for me simply because it was such a grace to be there.

The principal celebrant of the Liturgy was Patriarch Pimen, head of the Russian Orthodox Church. He is old and frail. Like all Orthodox bishops, he is a monk. His is a quiet and compassionate face, a face that has known suffering, perhaps knows suffering now. It is rumoured he was a prisoner in the 1930s.

It's a very large church, one of forty-seven "working" churches in Moscow, and was crowded as a church in the west would be on a major feast day. "But on a major feast," Tanya said, "you would have to come many hours early just to get inside." As in all Orthodox churches, believers pray standing up. For the non-initiated, this can be painful, as the liturgy runs about three hours. "The first hour, you think of how difficult it is to stand," Archbishop Pitirim told me. "The second hour you think of nothing at all. And the third hour you have wings."

It is active prayer. Some cross themselves and then bow slightly every few minutes, others cross themselves almost continually. I thought of the patterns the wind makes blowing across a field of wheat as I watched the rippling of bowing heads in the tightly packed congregation.

All the while the most beautiful singing was going on, mainly from two choirs facing each other in balconies on either side of the church. For some sections of the Liturgy, the congregation joined with the choirs, singing with great force.

While the congregation prayed, a steady flow of objects was passed forward hand-to-hand: folded bits of paper containing requests for prayer candles directed to particular icons, flowers, and a loaf of bread wrapped in paper. All these were accepted by two nuns who stood near the iconostasis.

The nuns wore black habits with circular hats and simple veils. One looked quite severe, the other had a face warm as a muffin. The muffin nun kept busy taking out the stumps of burned out candles and putting in new ones.

At first I stood like a wooden statue. I wanted to do what those around me were doing, not simply to fit in but because the body language of prayer seemed just the thing to do in a church, so much more interesting than simply standing there. But I felt awkward and ridiculous. I had my hands behind my back, like someone looking at paintings in a museum. Tanya whispered, "Let your hands hang at your side!" Soon enough I was doing my best to pray in the Russian style. (A Swedish friend, Margareta Ingelstam, who belongs to a non-demonstrative reformed church, had the experience of being lectured in Russian by a babushka who wouldn't rest until Margareta crossed herself and bowed. It seemed the old woman was saying to her, "This isn't the zoo and we aren't on exhibition. Do what we are doing or go away!")

I found myself alternating between praying and watching those around me. Many of my neighbours were babushkas, the older Russian women with shawls or knitted hats whose faces reveal indomitable souls. But there many were younger women, men of all ages, and quite a sprinkling of children. The babushkas were certainly the majority, but they had a lot of company. Seeing how many young people there were, I could understand the anxieties which, a few days ago, prompted *Pravda* to call for higher quality atheist propaganda in order to counter the growth of religious belief among the young.

What cannot be described is the tangible quality of the prayer in the church. I felt that if the walls and pillars of the church were taken away, the roof would rest securely on the faith of the congregation below. I have very rarely experienced this kind of intense spiritual presence. Was it always so in Russia? It must have been solid faith indeed to have survived many hard years and martyrdoms.

On the way out of the cathedral, we found ourselves in a crowd of families waiting to have their children baptized. A few months ago a pastor from Leningrad whom I met at a meeting in London estimated that the number of practicing members of the Orthodox Church in Russia had grown by ten-million in the past decade. He isn't a tall man. "But," he said, "short as I am, when it was just me and the babushkas, I was a tree among shrubs. But now I am just one more bush. The young people are the trees."

In the evening, I walked down Kalinin Prospekt, stopped for a while in a large record shop, gazed through various other shop windows, walked around the Kremlin walls, and finally rode the Metro, stopping at various stations as I did last year. The Metro still surprises me with the wide variety of styles. One station, Park Kulturi, has bas-reliefs of dancers, skaters, acrobats, all without a trace of political content. Komsomolskaya station, on the other hand, is intensely political. Its mosaics celebrate revolution, including America's. There is a large mosaic of George Washington on horseback that would fit right into any public building in Washington, DC.

October 23:

I talked about Soviet films and film makers with Victoria Reuter, a young translator on the staff of the Soviet Peace Committee. Though she is working for a secular organization, I noticed that she wears a small gold cross around her neck. She was surprised that I had seen *Moscow Doesn't Believe in Tears* and didn't know it had received an Oscar. "I have the impression," she said, "that films from our country aren't shown in the United States. But American films are very popular here. My favourites are *Kramer vs Kramer* and *Tootsie*. These were real hits in Moscow." Vicky, a great fan of Barbra Streisand, was envious that I had seen *Yentl*, which hasn't been imported to the Soviet Union. I promised to send her a tape of the music.

A recent Soviet film that Vicky recommended is *Life and Tears and Love*, about an old-age home. "The residents are waiting to die," Vicky said, "and in a way they are already dead. They are letting the dust settle on them. Then a new doctor joins the staff and is so alive, so interested in them, that he lifts them out of their passivity and depression and brings them back to life. It's a kind of resurrection story."

Another recent film she found quite special was *The Scarecrow*. "The word can also mean 'The Gargoyle,' " she explained. "There is a fantastic girl in it, eleven or twelve, a future Juliet. It's about children and misunderstanding and how cruel children can be to their friends."

In the evening I went to a Moscow theatre for children where a production of *The Humpbacked Pony* was being staged. Fine dancing and stunning sets. The humpbacked pony has the gift of flight. In one scene the pony and his rider fly across a stage covered with clouds broken only by church cupolas that dance around them.

October 24:

Vicky mentioned a singer whose voice and style have given her a national reputation for being a Russian Joan Baez: Jeanne Bichevskaya. "Do you think Joan Baez would ever come to sing in the Soviet Union? I know she is very critical of our country." Vicky has been the road manager for a number of western musicians travelling in the Soviet Union, including Harry Belafonte, but she found it too hard living so much of the year out of a suitcase.

At an afternoon meeting with the Religious Circles Commission of the Soviet Peace Committee, Nina Bobrova, director of the Women's Division of the External Church Affairs Department, spoke about the growing emphasis on peace in preaching in Russian churches.

"Sermons today include not only an explanation of the day's Bible text," she said, "but there is a definite emphasis on peacemaking. It is something that pastors think about. This is similar to what we see happening in churches in other parts of the world. When you visit our churches, you experience this, and the hospitality people give in their homes and churches in their hope and striving for peace. I see this happening in the United States as well. Things have changed a lot in both countries in the last few years! Four years ago I was a guest of Church Women United in the United States, and I remember there were people shocked to have a Soviet woman present at their meeting. They were actually very suspicious. Just who was I really speaking for? Maybe the KGB! Now when I go there it is entirely different."

And yet, she said, there are many things which haven't changed, even in the churches where there is much talk about peace and where guests from the Soviet Union are welcome. "I still find people in American churches speaking of Russians

17

as 'the enemy.' We in the Soviet Union must be loved, they say, because Jesus said, 'Love your enemy.' This word 'enemy' has connotations of hatred and opposition and means that in fact we threaten America. When we say 'friendship,' this has entirely different connotations. For us it would be truer to say, 'Love thy friend!' Here ordinary people, strange as it may sound to you, do not regard Americans as their enemy.''

Another participant in the meeting, Archdeacon Vladimir Nazarkin, suggested that we need to look more at the dark side of Christian history. ''Christ means peace. The Gospel is a message of peace. But we have to ask ourselves why this message has been so often ignored. Why has fascism emerged from Christian countries? Christians have played a big part in war, even talked about holy wars. We have often committed the sin of division. Now believers begin to understand that our faith leads us to overcome such division, but steps taken by Christians in the Soviet Union are often regarded by Christians in the west only as propaganda actions.''

Diana Francis, President of the International Fellowship of Reconciliation, had come to Moscow from Bath for these meetings with the Soviet Peace Committee. She responded with a comment about the problem of patriotism in her own country. ''It would not be charitable to say a British bishop consciously puts allegiance to Queen and country before allegiance to the Gospel. In fact we see all too often how patriotism takes priority over the Gospel. Yet there are examples of it *not* happening, as when the church service in St. Paul's Cathedral in London after the Falklands war was made a service of repentance rather than of celebration.''

Tomorrow we drive north-east of Moscow to Zagorsk, regarded as the living centre of the Russian Orthodox Church.

October 25:

The Holy Trinity — St. Sergius Lavra! After an hour's drive through woods and villages, our small IFOR group walked through a wide gate in the monastery's fortress walls, entering an enclave of monastic churches which has been the heart of Russian Orthodoxy for centuries. In ancient times this land was heavily forested. In 1354 St. Sergius of Radonez and his small community of fellow monks made a clearing where they built a church. A biographer in the next generation wrote, "St. Sergius built the Church of the Holy Trinity as a mirror for his community, that through gazing at the Unity, they might overcome the hateful divisions of this world." In 1422, twenty-four years after his death, a cathedral church dedicated to the Holy Trinity was built and Rublev's icon of the Trinity was painted for the iconostasis. (The original is now at the Tretyakov Gallery in Moscow; a remarkably good copy stands in its place.)

Every morning of the year, monks begin a service of prayer here, but pilgrims soon start to arrive and before long they take over the service, which continues without interruption until nightfall. The Slavonic chant begs the prayers of St. Sergius. It is a dark church, the only light coming from candles clustered near several icons and especially near the tomb of the saint.

The church and monastery were closed from 1930 until 1943, when Stalin's campaign against the Church ceased and many churches and religious institutions were allowed to re-open. At that time, the seminary of the Moscow Patriarchate, also here, re-opened, and worship resumed in the churches as the monastic community returned.

Our guide was a monk of the community, Fr. Alepia,

named for the first icon painter, he said, though this is not his own calling.

We paused at a chapel-like structure built over a well. The water, which began to flow miraculously during the lifetime of St. Sergius, has been associated with healing. I drank a cupful. It tasted like melted snow.

We went on to the seminary, a large building on the north side of the monastery. It includes a small museum which contains a remarkable collection of icons dating from a thousand years ago to those being painted at Zagorsk today. "Christianity gave the world the idea that death is an assumption, the lifting of the soul into heaven," we were told while standing before an icon of the Resurrection. "Christians wait for the spring of their bodies. Icons show what is eternal, the inner, sacred sense of what is happening. The icon is the Gospels in paint."

In the last room of the museum there were nineteenth-century paintings by the Itinerants, all of them masterpieces. What a pity these canvases are so little known.

A painting by Vasili Surikov shows Jesus healing the eyes of a blind beggar. The man stares in joyous astonishment at the world suddenly unveiled while his hands are bathed in light. Fr. Alepia pointed out a woman's face in the shadow over the arm with which Jesus is touching the man's head. "It is the face of Surikov's wife," Fr. Alepia told us. "When she died Surikov experienced such grief that he lost the will to paint. This was the first work he did after her death. The face Jesus is touching is Surikov's." While Jesus' hands are on Surikov, his eyes are on the viewer, as if to say, "I long to heal your eyes also." There is a quality of silent, timeless encounter. Surikov's work makes a bridge between Russian iconography and western painting.

A painting by Mikail Nesterov centres on a large icon of the crucifixion standing in the open, with woodland and a river behind it. To the left are common people in prayer. There are three people to the right: the writer Gogol on his knees at the foot of the cross, and behind him Fyodor Dostoyevsky and his wife, Anna Snitkina. In her arms is a small blue casket containing the body of their infant child. "Dostoyevsky and Gogol," said Fr. Alepia, "were among the few authors of their generation who turned toward the Orthodox faith while others went in the direction of secularism and atheism. But their writings have had profound consequences for the spiritual life of many people."

Vasili Polenov shows Jesus walking the paths above the Sea of Galilee. It is an intensely realistic portrait. Jesus, without a halo or any indication of divinity, seems to have paused for a moment. Staff in hand, from shadowed eyes he gazes from the painting, which has the effect of an icon. (Polenov, who lived until 1927, was among the first to receive the title of People's Artist.)

Another late nineteenth century painting, shows a young monk looking in alarm toward a chained door in the stone church. "This monk is shown painting an icon during the time of the iconoclasts," Fr. Alepia said. "In the eighth and ninth centuries, certain theologians in the Byzantine Empire declared that the veneration of icons was a form of idolatry. At times this was the view of the Emperor. There were two periods when icon painting was prohibited. To make a holy image could cost one's life. In the eighth century, during the bitterest period of iconoclasm, St. John of Damascus, living at the Mar Saba Monastery in the desert near Jerusalem, wrote his defence of Orthodox veneration of images. St. John argued that, because the Second Person of the Holy Trinity became flesh and was visible, he can be represented visually. It is a consequence of the Incarnation."

The monk's face in the painting could belong to anyone living through a period of repression who dreads the unexpected knock on the door. It is striking that in the first room of this small museum there is a model of the catacombs, and in the last room a painting of a more another period of martyrdom. "The purpose of art," our guide had said, "is to lead us from what can be seen to what cannot be seen." It also says what cannot be said.

Archimandrite Benedict received us in his office for lunch. We talked about the canons of iconography and what space there was within them for individual creativity. "Rublev is an example of what an individual can do, even within the limits and norms of icon painting. The icon presents special problems and requirements, but these should not be suffocating. One can paint from the Gospels in a different way, very successfully. And there are other kinds of religious paintings — for example Surikov's painting of Christ opening the eyes of the blind man."

The Seminary and Academy (the seminary's graduate school) have been growing. "The number of pupils has doubled in ten years. At present there are five hundred students, and a new enlargement is in preparation. Also the seminary has eight hundred non-resident students taking courses by correspondence. About ninety students each year are ordained to the priesthood. Together with the ordinations from the seminaries in Leningrad and Odessa, the Church receives about two hundred new priests each year. Believe me, with seven thousand Orthodox parishes, there is no unemployment for the clergy!" (The joke is, as one hears so often, that there is no unemployment in the Soviet Union.)

Fr. Benedict spoke about the simplicity of the Gospel: "Christ taught a way that is very simple. For example, he said, 'don't treat another as you don't want to be treated.' It is not so easy to do this, but it is a teaching that a child can understand."

Diana responded by mentioning the rather non-childish way of churches in their relations with political authorities. "This is not at all a simple question," Fr. Benedict commented, "though one can see in history some of the mistakes that churches make. At times the churches have suffered from the sin of envy, including envying power. Whoever is possessed by envy cannot be a peacemaker."

"Despair can also make us fail," Diana pointed out. "We need to share with each other our faith and vision, the vision such as Isaiah had of the peaceable kingdom."

"Yes," Fr. Benedict agreed, "we need to translate this into a vision of our time. The words of Isaiah give courage and hope, and that's peace! It is peace when the wolf dwells with the lamb. It is peace if we will translate these words into action, if we are active with these words. Christianity shows a way to overcome the sin of division. It is a peacemaking religion. The first century Christians did not kill. They knew that we are one people. The highest thing is to be human. 'The glory of God is the human person fully alive,' one of the Church Fathers taught. Nothing is more precious. And what happiness it is to meet one who can give consolation in difficult times, and who can show us how to be patient in the things we don't like in each other. Those who can do this are truly following the law of love. To struggle for peace, you must start with yourself. If a person will find out and understand that he's wrong, he won't be able to think of himself as better or higher than others. Then you understand that each person is on the way to perfection, struggling along the way, and making mistakes, but still enduring. Whoever thinks he has made no mistakes either hasn't done anything, or is not sincere.''

October 26:

This afternoon our little IFOR group met with Archbishop Platon at the offices of Department for External Church Affairs, a low wooden building of the sort that has largely been destroyed in the modernization of Moscow.

The most animated moment with him was occasioned by a question about the large painting that hangs at one end of the conference room where he received us. In it a hostile figure in gold robes, but with a dark outer cloak, is regarding a bishop with rage. The bishop stands with great calm, looking up as if he were considering an icon on the church wall. Between these two figures is a third, a flunkey type, appealing to the bishop with a gesture that seems to say, "Take care! Say Say yes! Your life depends on it!"

"The man in gold," said Archbishop Platon, "is Ivan the Terrible. The bishop is Metropolitan Philip of Moscow. Ivan entered the church under cover of a monk's cloak to demand that the Metropolitan cease speaking out against the czar's policies. The Metropolitan refused. Later Ivan had him arrested and finally the czar had Philip strangled in his prison cell. Philip is one of the saints of our church."[7]

An interesting painting for any church leader anywhere in the world to consider. Last year I sat in meetings in this same room for four days, occasionally looking at this painting yet giving it little thought. It has taken time to discover how much the Orthodox say through images rather than words.

7. George P. Fedotov, *St. Filipp: Metropolitan of Moscow* (Belmont, MA: Nordland Publishing Co., 1978).

October 27:

I was able to stop in for another evening visit with Archbishop Pitirim. He mentioned the class he had just met with at the seminary in Zagorsk.

"We were discussing the Kingdom of Heaven. I asked what does the Gospel say about the Kingdom of Heaven? They told me that Christ came to earth to invite everyone to heaven. His method was first to do miracles and only then to explain why he did them. But modern humanity is tired of explanations — they are not enough. I asked the students what they will do as priests. They gave various answers, none of which I found very interesting. The answer should be, I said, 'I will do miracles.' But what kind of miracles? The miracle of change! The miracle of changing our habits. The miracle of changing ourselves. We need to be changed in such a way that people can come to God through us. The great miracle is to change ourselves and to show in our own lives that the heaven of God is real."

October 28:

Having arrived at the gate to the Novodevichy Monastery a little early, Tanya and I walked down the hillside along a path by the monastery walls to a riverside park. We watched a father and his daughter feed swans, one white swan, one black. Mothers pushed small children in strollers, stopping to talk with each other. The park is a popular place for runners. Groups of them regularly came down the path by the monastery wall, waving their arms as if they hoped to take wing at the water's edge, then going round the corner of the monastery walls, stopping to do some exercises while standing in a circle. If I lived in Moscow, this park would draw me often.

We were joined at the monastery gate by Tatiana Volgina, a member of Archbishop Pitirim's staff who is involved with English-language publications. She introduced us to Olga Kurbatova, a historian who for eighteen years has been working at the Novodevichy Monastery. Olga is large, round-faced, with lively eyes, her hair pulled back in a bun. She possesses an immense, contagious enthusiasm that pours out in animated talk and frequent laughter. It was love at first sight. What a privilege it would be to see all of Russia in Olga's company. I am far from her only admirer. Archbishop Pitirim calls her Sister Barbara because of her discovery of an ancient icon of St. Barbara under the paint of a more recent one.

The monastery was built in 1524 to house a particular icon that came to Russia from Byzantium. This was the Smolensk Mother of God, so named because it was in the Cathedral of Smolensk until it came to Moscow at the time of the union of Moscow and Smolensk. The icon's history is painted on the wall of the main church but the original icon is no longer here.

The monastery is similar to Zagorsk though on a smaller scale. In one of its churches, worshippers gather twice daily. There is no longer a monastic community here, but the monastery houses the residence and offices of Metropolitan Yuvenali, vicar of the diocese of Moscow under the Patriarch.

In czarist times Novodevichy was mainly for women from noble families. "For example," Olga explained, "when a noble woman was widowed, it would be a disgrace either to remarry or to continue living in the civil world, so she would come here. Of course unmarried girls came also. Whoever came brought all their valuables so it became very rich in lands and was magnificently decorated. When the Patriarch of Antioch visited, he declared that he had not seen another monastery so rich or noble as this one. The best artists of the time, in the Moscow region, worked here. It was here that Boris Gudounov was made czar. If you see the opera, *Boris Gudounov*, the first scene is here."

The monastery figures in the rise of Peter the Great and the decline of his sister Sophia, who had been regent ten years, until Peter was seventeen and ordered her into the Novodevichy. It was outside these walls that Peter had scaffolds erected and executed some of the *streltsy*, Kremlin guards who had turned against Peter and whom he suspected wanted to put Sophia in power.

"In the hands of one of those who were hung," Olga said, "a charter was placed appealing to Sophia to return to the throne. Peter was good at practical jokes, but often rather grim ones. Some years later, when Peter's second wife was the object of too much attention from someone in the court, Peter had the man beheaded in Red Square, with his wife as a witness. When she returned to her room she found the man's head in pickling solution in a jar on a table in her bedroom."

Olga pointed out how those who built the monastery organized the main work within a pattern that follows the lines of the cross, in the process abandoning some earlier traditions. "In Sophia's time, many artists and stone masons worked here. New walls were made in the Moscow baroque style, buildings of red and white stone. There were private chambers built for the czar's use when he came to visit, and a private chapel, which you see over the main gate, and which is a living church again. The architects of the seventeenth century, confronted with difficult tasks here, created something new within these walls, making it one of the glories of Russia.''

We spent some time in the Cathedral of the Assumption, a "summer church" with five cupolas now in the midst of restoration, then went to the smaller church still used for daily services. It is called a "winter church" because, with its low ceiling and absence of cupolas, it can be kept warm in cold weather. Then we went on to the large cemetery where many notable Muscovites are buried: writers, artists, actors, dancers, musicians, war heroes, generals and admirals, an astronaut, and one former General Secretary of the Communist Party.

Olga pointed out a low stone bench where Stalin used to sit before the grave of his wife, Nadezhda Alliluyeva, who had opposed his brutal policies until her suicide in 1932. Standing before another grave, where Nikita Khrushchev is buried, Olga mentioned that the sculptor who had designed the monument had gone into exile. "How he survives in exile I cannot imagine," she said. "For me, I count the days whenever I am away from Moscow, even though I am still in Russia. I cannot think of a worse fate than not being able to live here."

Before we left the cemetery, Olga told a joke about a man who more than anything wanted to be buried in the Novodevichy Cemetery. Finally he found a high official who said he would try and do something to help. The next day the official called back. "Yuri, you're in luck! There is a place for you, but you must hurry. Your grave is available tomorrow only."

FEBRUARY 1987

The agreement made with Archbishop Pitirim in 1984 nearly died on the vine. It took longer than I imagined to find publishers in the US and Britain who would commit themselves to the project, a pre-condition from my side. In the spring of 1985, I was away in Jerusalem for three months, a sabbatical leave which I spent studying Russian history and Orthodoxy and leading a seminar on peacemaking at the Institute for Ecumenical Research at Tantur, near Jerusalem. In the spring of 1986, Crossroad/ Continuum in the US and Marshall Pickering in Britain agreed to publish the book, but I heard nothing from Moscow about when I might return. Then in October 1986, while in Copenhagen for a World Peace Congress, I met Metropolitan Yuvenali, vicar of the Moscow diocese of the Russian Orthodox Church. He and I had been asked to give the opening speeches to the Congress' religious section. We talked at some length between sessions. I mentioned my book project and asked if he could help push things along. Before parting we exchanged rosaries, in his case one of black silk that had come from Jerusalem, in my case a rosary that had been given to me by Pope John Paul II. Two months later I received an invitation from him to take part in the religious section of a Peace Forum to be held in Moscow in February. After the Forum, he said, further travel within the USSR would be possible.

Moscow, February 12, 1987:

I'm staying in the Mezhdunarodnaya, an un-American name for an otherwise very American hotel, designed by an American architect, fitted with American Standard plumbing, and with glass-walled American Otis elevators that offer a dramatic view of a cavernous gardened lobby. The idea was to make foreign businessmen feel at home in Moscow. The Mezhdunarodnaya — it means international — is part of a complex of modern conference and convention buildings. The Russian Orthodox Church normally puts up its guests in the Hotel Ukraina across the river, a cheaper place with an old-shoes feeling altogether lacking here, where the religious section of the Moscow Peace Forum is to be held.

On the television news programme tonight, there are clips of famous people arriving for the Peace Forum: movie stars, authors, generals, scientists, and a Nobel Prize winning doctor from America. This was followed by a recitation of the temperatures in principal cities of the Soviet Union: 45 degrees *above* zero in Tashkent, 25 degrees *below* zero in Murmansk. I suppose there is no other country that records a 70-degree temperature spread at a given hour of the day. Within the Soviet Union's eleven times zones, it is normal. The news was followed by a British movie, "Passage to India," starring a Russian-speaking Alec Guinness.

Moscow, February 13:

There are about a thousand people in Moscow for the Peace Forum, divided up into various sections — religious, scientific, medical, literary, artistic, business, ecological, military. The religious and business sections of the Forum are meeting in this hotel.

Georgi Derevianchenko, Assistant to the Chairman of the External Church Affairs Department of the Moscow Patriarchate, has asked me how long I can stay after the Forum and what places I would like to visit. I proposed Leningrad, Novgorod, Pskov, Suzdal and Vladimir, with a possible return visit to the Holy Trinity Lavra in Zagorsk. "No problem!" said Georgi. "The only thing is I have to see who I can find to travel with you."

This afternoon, having waded through the snow to a bookshop on Kalinin Prospekt, I met an economist. We have beards in common, a rarity in Moscow, though his is more neatly trimmed than mine. He had an elegant manner and, now that I think of it, resembled the last czar, Nicholas II. We talked about art books — I had just bought a very handsome one reproducing paintings by Ilya Repin.

I asked him about *glasnost*, wondering whether he would dare to talk politics in the busy entrance area of a crowded shop in the middle of Moscow. Not a blink of hesitation. He did little pantomimes of the last few Soviet leaders prior to Gorbachev. He showed Brezhnev as a man with head tilted heavily to one side, eyes half-closed. "Corruption prospered," he said. "It was worse than you can imagine. Then came Brezhnev's successors, corpses even while still in office, and and nothing changed." He played the part of one dead body, then another, eyes now entirely closed. Then, springing back to life, "But Gorbachev, now he is alive and he is a clever

31

man. Finally we have someone who is alive and can think."

He talked about the impending publication of Pasternak's long-suppressed *Dr. Zhivago*, and mentioned various films I should see, especially *Repentance*, which has escaped from the censors and is showing in cinemas all over the country, including seventeen Moscow theatres. It is the first time that Stalin's era has been the object of a critical movie. "Stalin simply disappeared," the economist said. "One day his picture was on every wall. The next day it was gone. Until Khrushchev, nothing was said about Stalin or what he did or how many died or where they died, and after Khrushchev, the silence returned. Now research into the Stalin period is finally being allowed." Our conversation drifted on to the topic of used book shops in Moscow. We parted company after exchanging addresses.

Moscow, February 14:

The Forum was off and running as of this morning. Metropolitan Yuvenali is chairing the religious section. About two hundred are taking part, mainly Christians but a good many Jews, Hindus, Buddhists, Shintoists and Moslems. Lots of journalists and photographers were on hand for the opening session but few, if any, from the west.

After several hours of opening speeches in the plenary session, we broke into several smaller sections in which nothing was planned. Those chairing the meetings (in our case Bill Thompson, a former head of the Presbyterian Church in the United States) presided very lightly. Most of the speeches were off-the-cuff and, on the whole, either interesting or mercifully brief.

Several speakers touched on hot subjects, including Afghanistan, where what the USSR is doing was compared to what America did in Vietnam. Remarkably, no Russians stood up to say, "Wait a minute, please stop these cold war speeches. Soviet troops are in Afghanistan because they were invited in by an ally. They are merely defending a democratic government against counter-revolutionaries armed and paid by the CIA." This is a speech I have often heard. What was said by Russians boiled down to: "It was a tragic mistake and our government is committed to getting out. But we can't just pack our bags and fly away." (This was what one heard in the US during the last part of the Vietnam war, just before Americans packed their bags and flew away.)

One church leader from the US spoke about religious repression in the USSR and suggested specific changes in the Soviet Constitution. An older Russian priest rose to ask how Americans would respond to proposals from Soviet citizens advocating changes in the American Constitution. But he didn't make any claims that all was well for believers in the USSR nor did he remind us of human rights violations in the United States.

It is remarkable how little America-bashing there has been. The Russians stress theological aspects of peacemaking. They seem less "political" than those coming from the west, except that they mention disarmament initiatives the USSR has taken and express the hope that there can be a positive response to them.

After supper I had a long talk with a translator who is taking part in the business section of the Peace Forum. A Muscovite, he talked about the struggle in the city to save and restore old buildings. Then we switched gears to Russian literature, starting with Dostoyevsky and working our way to Valentin Rasputin, a contemporary author whose stories often have a religious note and who is well known for his struggle to protect the environment from industrialism. Then he asked if I knew the books of Thomas Merton. It turns out he is a great fan of Merton and has a number of Merton books in his library. He was surprised that I had actually known Merton, but not nearly as surprised as I was that Merton's books can be found on Moscow bookshelves.

Moscow, Sunday, February 15:

Participants in the religious section of the Forum went to the Danilov — St. Daniel — Monastery, a few miles south of the Kremlin, to take part in the Holy Liturgy. A community of twenty-one monks is now living there. It is the youngest monastic community in the USSR, though residing in Moscow's oldest monastery. When it was founded in 1282 by St. Prince Daniel, the monastery was in the countryside where it doubled as a fortress and place of refuge in case of attack. The Church hopes to have sixty monks in residence by the time restoration work is finished in the summer of 1988.

After the Revolution, the Danilov became an orphanage, then an institution for juvenile delinquents, and more recently a factory. The ancient grandeur was worn away until it became a grim, dilapidated compound with the atmosphere of a prison. In 1983, in a surprising gesture by the state, the compound was returned to the Russian Orthodox Church. The derelict buildings are now experiencing a resurrection. Hundreds of tons of rubble and mud have been carted away, hard labour mainly carried out by devout volunteers. On every side there are signs of the work in progress, though none today, a Sunday. Cobble stones, bricks and lumber are heaped against the walls while several buildings are draped in scaffolding. The towering main gate has been painted a bright raspberry pink. Two of the churches are fully restored. The abbot's residence, serving also as a reception centre, looks like new. There is a residence for the monks. Another completed building houses the External Church Affairs Department of the Moscow Patriarchate.

The Liturgy was in the Holy Trinity Cathedral, a cruciform church from the era of Peter the Great that reflects his preference for western church design. Local people were mostly on the far side of the church, with guests from the Forum on the other. Chairs had been brought in for us, on the assumption that we wouldn't survive hours of standing. I felt odd at the thought of sitting in an Orthodox Church and managed to escape the chairs, and so had a good vantage point on the steps by the iconostasis for watching the vesting of Metropolitan Filaret of Kiev, the principal celebrant.

The singing burst on us like sudden rain shower: *gospodi pomilui!* "Lord, have mercy on us." It is the most often repeated prayer in Orthodox worship.

I remember Thomas Merton sitting on the porch steps of his hermitage at the Abbey of Gethsemani in Kentucky in 1962 and explaining that the mass is a kind of dance. Were he here, perhaps he would agree that in the Orthodox Church the mass is a ballet. I felt as if I had a box seat at the Bolshoi. Two deacons on either side of Metropolitan Fileret assisted him in the slow, graceful layering of his body with special garments. Each item was individually blessed, each was put on slowly, with the utmost gravity and grace. It was like watching a surgeon being prepared for open-heart surgery. Every motion seemed essential. This multitude of preparatory actions, a slow-motion avalanche of little symbols, forms a kind of visual litany drawing one into sacred space. They also suggest that even the most minor action, the most hidden gesture, can be a moment of standing in God's presence.

A family was directly across from me on the far side of the iconostasis. I was enchanted by two young sisters, perhaps five and seven years old, and their young brother, about four. The boy was sitting on the floor, back resting against the iconostasis, sucking his thumb very cheerfully, paying occasional attention to what was going on. The girls were deeply absorbed in the Liturgy, watching everything, crossing themselves solemnly without a trace of self-consciousness. At times the younger girl leaned back against her older sister, who in turn had her arms around the younger one. At other times they were holding hands.

A short distance away I noticed a lean man about my age, also bearded, with his wife and their son, about nine years

36

old. The intelligence in the boy's face and his attitude of deep devotion were impressive. He often rested against his father.

All the while the singing fell on us as if we were standing under a waterfall.

There is a Russian phrase — *bytovoe blagochestie* — which means "the art of ritual living."[1] This has to do with both rituals and images rooted in the centre of life, community life and private life. To grow more at ease in the art of ritual living is to discover the possibility of living every moment aware that one really is a Temple of the Holy Spirit, a "bearer of the Divine image," as the Orthodox put it so often.

I thought of the art of ritual living late yesterday afternoon when I paused to visit a church on a busy Moscow street. Some of the people walking by paused, bowed, crossed themselves, at home with the gestures, though a Metro station was just in back of them and many others streamed by without a glance at the church. There seemed to be no embarrassment, and no sense of display either, in those whose religious belief is obviously at the heart of their lives. In fact I am the sort of person who would like to use these gestures, and here I can do so without anyone paying any attention, but I don't dare to do the same in Amsterdam or New York, or even Rome.

Coming out of the church after the Liturgy at the Danilov Monastery, I found a crowd of people waiting for a smaller monastery church to open its doors. Bells were being rung. A light snow was falling.

I happened to be standing along the path of Patriarch Pimen at lunchtime. He has aged since I last saw him two years ago. Now he has difficulty walking. Even with two people helping him as he came into the restaurant and walked to his place at the table, it was slow going and obviously painful, yet his lively eyes were darting around with great attention, not missing a thing. Once we were seated, he gave a speech that was quite brisk.

Participants in the religious section of the Forum met in

1. Nicolas Zernov, *The Russians and Their Church,* 3rd ed. (Crestwood, NY: St. Vladimir's Seminary Press, 1978), p. 106.

the late afternoon to hear the draft text of a proposed common statement. It was the work of a committee that included Dwain Epps, a tall, strapping American employed on the staff of the National Council of Churches in New York City. The committee managed to catch the spirit of the meeting, neither accusing nor praising but concentrating on positive steps to be taken. "People of religion have special roles to play, among them: promoting unity among the peoples; increasing contacts across lines of division; improving the spiritual and devotional life of human communities; helping to eliminate prejudiced enemy images; and intensifying education for peace."

Added to these few points for religious believers was an appeal to leaders of the nuclear states calling for them to renounce nuclear deterrence, respect the existing Anti-Ballistic Missile Treaty (thus not to militarize space), and proceed to conclude new treaties that are concrete steps toward a nuclear-free world. It was a simple text, but not lacking in a sense of urgency: "We appeal to all to commit themselves unalterably to the task of building the basis for common security today. The time has come for us to ask the ancient questions: If not me, who? If not now, when?"

Moscow, February 16:

The final gathering brought all the Forum participants together for a plenary meeting at the Kremlin. Our first stop was the Palace of Facets in the most ancient part of the Kremlin, a large hall decorated with Biblical scenes of the creation of the world — suitable images for a meeting preoccupied with threats to creation. This was once the czar's throne room. After an hour of informal conversation, we were ushered into the Supreme Soviet.

There was nothing hierarchical about seating arrangements. More than half-way back in the hall, I found myself sitting directly in front of a member of the Central Committee of the Communist Party, Georgi Arbatov, director of the Institute for US-Canada Studies. Over to the side I noticed Kris Kristofferson, star of the American television series, "Amerika," a film dramatizing a Russian take-over of the United States. He looked rather sheepish. Not many rows in front of us was Andrei Sacharov, about whom the press gathered as if he were Marilyn Monroe risen from the dead, and truly it was startling that a man so long kept in internal exile was now an honoured guest in the Kremlin. Sitting at a podium in the front of the hall were representatives from each section of the Forum, plus Gorbachev.

One highlight of this final session was a speech by Graham Greene, representing the writers' section. He apologized that he would be speaking just for himself but, he commented, "no writer can possibly represent more than one writer." Then he explained, without ever mentioning his last novel, what that novel — *Monsignor Quixote* — was all about: religious people opening their ears to Marxists about a just social order, and Marxists discovering that God not only exists but is far more radical than they are. Greene said that the East-West conflict

39

pre-dates the Bolshevik Revolutions of 1917, having its roots in "a certain suspicion, an enmity even, between the Roman Catholic Church and Communism." ("And long before the Communists, the Catholics hated the Orthodox," the Russian sitting next to me whispered.) Greene thought that in Latin America, "except among a few Catholics nearly as old as I am," this enmity is being broken down as Marxists and Christians make common cause in attempting to build a more just social order. "The dream I have is that this cooperation between Catholics and Communists will spread and prolong itself in Europe, East and West." It was his prayer, he said, despite his advanced years, to live long enough to see "a Soviet ambassador giving good advice at the Vatican."

General Michael Harbottle from Britain spoke, as did Dr. Bernard Lown of Harvard, one of the initiators of Physicians for the Prevention of Nuclear War. Paulos Mar Gregorios from India, a president of the World Council of Churches, spoke on behalf of the religious section of the Forum. There was an Italian businessman, a political scientist, an ecologist. The speeches, all broadcast live on Soviet television and rebroadcast in the evening, were quite good.

Gorbachev came last and gave a major address. He argued that the fact that we have survived forty years with nuclear weapons is a not something to bank on forever. We are the lucky survivors of many war-risking games of chance. Nuclear deterrence, he said, as "a policy based on intimidation and threat, must always be backed up with definite action, and thus actually increases the chances of military conflict." If we continue in the direction we are going, living in a constant state of high alert with enormous stocks of such weapons, then "catastrophe is highly likely . . . eventually we will terminate our own existence, and there will be no second Noahs."

He didn't agree with those who argue that war is part of human nature. "Many say so. If so we are doomed. I cannot accept such a dogma."

His basic message was that the responsibility is in our hands to make an unprecedented break not only with weapons of mass destruction but with militarism and all that it involves. Everything that matters depends on this.

Gorbachev is no pacifist, yet he seems to be an abolitionist: someone who believes in a future without doomsday weaponry and even a future in which war is as unthinkable as slavery. "The immortality of the human race has been lost and can only be regained by the elimination of nuclear weapons. The nuclear guillotine must be broken and with it the alienation of politics from ethics."

He spoke about democratization and the "revolution now in progress" in the USSR, which he said was unstoppable and which shouldn't be seen as simply a response to western pressures or criticisms but as an event with local roots. "We want a democratic society. We want more socialism and more democracy"

He said the main problem with politics is that it has become "soul-less." Gorbachev's own view seemed to be summed up in the words, "Life will have its way."

On the way out of the Supreme Soviet, a journalist from Reuters asked me what I thought of Gorbachev's speech. I said that words on a page or a face on a television screen just aren't the same as hearing someone speaking at length, unedited, and in the same room. I hoped she could find a way to communicate the possibility that what he says isn't a propaganda charade. His speech reminded me, I said, of Pope John XXIII's encyclical, *Pacem in Terris*

There was a buffet lunch on the top floor of the Palace of Congresses, the one modern building within the Kremlin. For the first time this week, we had wine with our meal. With Gorbachev in the room — both he and his wife Raissa were meeting Forum participants at one end of the room — it seemed his campaign against alcohol could be relaxed.

After getting close enough to Gorbachev to take a photo as requested by two of my daughters (they hold him in the same esteem they have for the singer, Madonna), I sought out Graham Greene, who was sipping a glass of white wine. He has pale watery eyes and a weak hand shake — he is eighty-two — but still a strong pulse in his words. He worried

41

that he had let rhetoric get the best of him during his speech. A Russian writer acting as Greene's guide mentioned that *Monsignor Quixote* is to be published in the USSR next year. If so, it will be the first book on Christian-Marxist dialogue, albeit in the form of a novel, ever published in the USSR.

I talked with actor Gregory Peck. We spoke about Dan Berrigan's play, "The Trial of the Catonsville Nine", which Peck had produced as a film fifteen years ago. It was a box-office disaster but won a film prize. Peck thinks one day it will come into its own. I noticed Yoko Ono standing quietly by herself, and saw Marcello Mastroianni, looking venerable and tired, cheerfully signing autographs.

In the afternoon I was one of several people accompanying Metropolitan Yuvenali to the United States Embassy. With us was a priest from the Leningrad Theological Academy, a Shintoist priest from Japan, a Canadian Dukhobor (the Christian pacifist sect that Tolstoy supported late in his life), and a translator. We were received in a small, dingy room on the ground floor. The Metropolitan didn't seem annoyed. In fact I was impressed by how warm and unpretentious he was. He asked the embassy staff to forward to President Reagan a copy of the final statement of the religious section of the Forum and the same medal — an enamelled medallion with a view of the earth from space — that had been presented to Gorbachev in the morning.

When the Soviet nuclear moratorium was mentioned, the embassy staff responded by recalling that, in the sixties, it was the USSR that had broken a nuclear moratorium that was being observed by both super-powers. But one of them said that the new developments in the USSR were bound, sooner or later, to have a positive effect on US policy.

Moscow, February 17:

Just before six I was picked up at the hotel by Boris Udovenko, a priest from Kiev with a greying beard who lived in Oxford for a year or two and speaks English fluently. We're to spend the next two weeks together.

We spent two sweaty, unforgettable hours participating in the vespers service at the Resurrection Church, a small parish a quarter-mile northwest of Red Square. I don't think that I have ever in my life been so jammed together with other people. Normally the church isn't quite so packed, I was told afterward, but this happened to be the Feast of Our Lady Help of Sinners. The feast days of Mary always mean crowded churches.

It was a struggle getting inside. Once there, it was impossible to move. I couldn't even raise or lower my arms. We were pressed together like match sticks, a young woman on my left, an old babushka on my right, an elderly man in front of me, and God knows who in back. Occasionally everyone would shift and in those moments I could move. There was a space when I got my camera out of my pocket, another space when I was able to raise it and take a few photos, but then a long wait before it was possible to lower my arm and put the camera back in my pocket. Being unable to sing the music or understand most of what was being sung, I alternated between silent prayer and simply watching people, while trying not to stare.

It is in prayer and love that the human face is most illumined and beautiful. There were so many faces that seemed transfigured. I noticed one woman with tears running down here cheeks, her lips trembling. She couldn't have raised her hands to wipe her eyes if she wanted to.

All the while the two choirs were singing, the professional

choir on the right, the amateur choir on the left. The parish has an international reputation. I had first heard about it from Fr. Alexis Voogd in Amsterdam whose daughter is studying choir direction at the seminary in Leningrad.

At times I closed my eyes and thought about nothing at all, not even about standing, as I was being held up by those around me and was carried by the music as a leaf is carried along on the surface of a stream.

Afterward we went to the residence of Metropolitan (he was promoted from Archbishop last month) Pitirim. After a prayer of blessing, we had a light supper of lenten pancakes — *blini* — with sour cream. Then Boris and I went to the train station.

On the train to Leningrad:

What is it about train travel that is so much more exciting than going by air? It was eleven when we got to the train station. We walked through heavy snow and clouds of steam until we found our car and then, after getting our bags inside, came out and stood in the snow until the train began to move. Two others from the Forum joined us for the trip to Leningrad, Milt Efthimiou, assistant to the Ecumenical Patriarchate of the Greek Orthodox Archdiocese in New York City, and Roger Williamson, an Englishman living in Uppsala, Sweden, where he directs the Life and Peace Institute. We squeezed together in one compartment to drink tea that was brought by the car attendant, very hot, in crystal glasses with silver filigree holders.

I asked Boris what prompted him to become a priest. "At first it wasn't that I wanted to become a priest, just that I wanted to be able to answer the questions my class-mates asked me. They knew my parents were believers, that we went to church. There was a certain amount of taunting and teasing, and sometimes very hard questions that I couldn't answer. So when I thought about college, I had the idea of applying for theological study. Luckily, I was accepted. I was in Leningrad four years. In 1958, when I graduated, I was almost sure that I wanted to be ordained. But it wasn't an easy choice. Even those who have been sure from the beginning of their studies hesitated at the last moment. It was the Khrushchev era, a hard time for our Church with many churches being closed. Some graduates of the seminary went into factory jobs. You didn't know what might happen. Also I had as yet no plans to marry and in our church you are either married — and this comes before ordination — or you are a monk. I admire monks but I knew I didn't want to be one! So all this

45

took some time. But a year later I was married — that was 1959 — and very soon after that I was ordained. And there are no regrets about either marriage or priesthood."

We sat talking for nearly an hour, sipping tea, watching the birch trees and the blur of snow caught in the light from the train.

Leningrad, February 18:

After a morning round of more scalding hot tea, we arrived in Leningrad at nine. A bright sky, brilliant light, and a lot of snow on the ground.

I can understand why visitors from the west feel especially at home here. Leningrad is simultaneously exotic and familiar. The city is an architectural rendering of Peter the Great's desire to shake off old Russia and to embrace the west. It looks like an idealized blending of Amsterdam, London, Rome and Venice as they were two hundred years ago: canals and wide avenues lined with long, low buildings of classic inspiration. The main colours are lemon white, pale green and creamy yellow. The fact that there are practically no signs or advertisements, except for the occasional political one, contributes to the city's unspoiled appearance. At least in the centre of the city, things are less crowded than they ever were in western Europe. There is no sign, at least in this part of town, of the grim sections described by Dostoyevsky in *Crime and Punishment*.

We had a glimpse of the pastel-hued Hermitage, formerly the Winter Palace of the Czars, on the far side of the Neva River. It looks like it was shipped in stone by stone from Versailles.

Directly across the street from the Moscow Hotel, where we are staying, is the St. Alexander Nevski Lavra. A lavra is a monastery of the highest order. There were four in pre-revolutionary Russia and now only one of them, the Holy Trinity Lavra in Zagorsk, is functioning. Still they refer to this one as a lavra. Perhaps one day it will be alive with monks again. The seminary is on the far side of the monastery grounds, nearly a mile away.

The lavra's principal church, the Holy Trinity Cathedral, remains open. Approaching it to take part in the morning

47

Liturgy, we joined a procession of people walking up the snow-covered road that passes through the lavra's chapel gate.

If one uses the ancient cathedrals in Moscow as a yardstick, this cathedral doesn't look at all Russian. It is a wonderful church to be in but, if I didn't know where I was, my first guess would be Rome. Even the iconostasis manages to look Italian.

The most impressive part of the cathedral is the least beautiful, the large crypt underneath where baptisms occur. About two hundred people a week — well over ten thousand a year — are baptized here. Baptisms alone would seem to be enough to keep the cathedral's six priests and three deacons fully occupied. One long passage way, freshly painted white, has been made into a waiting area with old couches lining the walls and icons of every period and style hanging above them.

After the Liturgy, a priest, who had been in seminary with Boris, met us and showed us around. Information for me was sandwiched in with news of friends with whom they had studied. Boris hasn't been in Leningrad in a long time. They had much catching up to do.

Despite the cold and the snow, we had a long leisurely walk in the cemetery adjacent to the monastery. As with the Novodevichy Monastery, in Moscow, or Westminster Abbey, in London, to be offered burial space here is among society's highest honours. Dostoyevsky's bust marks his grave, a place of constant pilgrimage even in icy weather. I waited for a crowd of Russians to leave before taking my turn, took off my warm fur hat and crossed myself in the Russian manner.

What a thing it would be to see all at once the hundreds of thousands, perhaps millions, of people who have gathered at Dostoyevsky's last resting place. One of the people who prayed here before me, nearly twenty years ago, was the founder of the Catholic Worker movement, Dorothy Day.[2] I felt as much in her company as in Dostoyevsky's.

2. Jim Forest, *Love Is the Measure: A Biography of Dorothy Day* (Mahwah, NJ: Paulist Press, and Basingstoke, England: Marshall Pickering, 1986). An account of her pilgrimage to Dostoyevsky's grave is included in the chapter "Further Travels," pp. 173 ff.

48

A few yards away are the monuments to the composers Tchaikovsky, Glinka, Rimsky-Korsakov and Borodin.

We went on to several working churches in different parts of the city. One church has a fence entirely made of cannons all pointing straight up. Fence building seems rather a good alternative use for weaponry: swords into plowshares. Before the revolution, the church was a military chapel. Now it serves the neighbourhood. No service was going on when we arrived, but the pastor was there, having just finished a funeral.

A few people were busy counting and packing thin amber candles of the sort that are placed in front of icons. Depending on size, candles sell for thirty kopecks to a ruble each, which isn't much but is far more than they cost to make. "This is the main way that the Russian Orthodox Church supports itself," Boris said. "There are many thousands of candles sold every day in churches around the country." Churches also sell small silk-screened icons, about ten rubles each. The greatest part of the sales price is a gift.

In the late afternoon, we went out to the Piskarioskoye Cemetery where most of the people who died during the siege of Leningrad are buried. In the course of nine hundred days, beginning in September 1941, 641,803 people perished. Although there were casualties as a result of the hundred thousand bombs and one hundred and fifty thousand artillery shells that rained on the city, the majority died of starvation or illnesses brought on by malnutrition. The highest death tolls, thousands per day, occurred during the terrible winter months of 1941-42, when the city, in record cold, was without heat and water. Weakened inhabitants simply froze to death on the streets and in their homes. It was usual to see corpses being hauled to the cemetery on small sleds. Students often had the job of bringing bodies out of the flats when no family member remained with the strength to do this. Although the very young and the elderly succumbed first, in the end the death rate knew no age limits.

A small museum next to the cemetery entrance allows the visitors a glimpse of life in Leningrad during the siege. Behind glass there is a piece of black bread and a ration card. Everyone got a two hundred and fifty-gram piece of bread each day. As one can see from the piece of bread here, part of the weight was sawdust. Next to the bread was a photo of a schoolgirl and some pages from her diary: "Our upstairs neighbour Ivan died last night." "Grandmother died this morning." "Mother died." "Father died." The one death she didn't record was her own.

There is an eternal flame burning at one end of the cemetery, a statue of a grieving woman — Mother Russia — at the other, and in between, mass graves marked only by the year of burial. Around the eternal flame, partly hidden in the snow, were thousands of flowers. We would have added a few ourselves, but just as we arrived, the flower stand had sold its last daffodil. It was sunset as we left, yet people were still arriving by car and bus—old people, young adults, school children.

I was a baby in America during the nine hundred-day siege. It is more than forty years since these deaths and yet there is this endless procession of mourners. I notice some visitors leave pieces of bread — bread that would have saved the starving.

Most of the people at this morning's Liturgy in the Holy Trinity Cathedral were older women, but at tonight's vesper service at St. Nicholas Cathedral there were nearly as many men. More surprising, a large part of the congregation was in its twenties. I continue finding it hard to stop watching people and simply to do what they are doing, which is praying.

Leningrad, February 19:

For visitors from the west, the Hermitage is Leningrad's major attraction. Imposing on the outside, it is truly stunning within. There are no mere rooms but rather hall after hall, all in the most ornate baroque style, every doorway opening into something quite different and amazing and huge. It is an experience of endless splendour and limitless wealth. Yet the limit was reached and the place did in fact change hands quite abruptly. I lingered on the stairway that had echoed with the shouts of Bolsheviks as they broke into this palace of gilded surfaces and vast mirrors on the night of November 7, 1917.

Most of these paintings were here when the revolutionaries took possession. The collection, then and now, is mainly western European. Many of the canvases are simply decorative work that would fit in well with feasts and balls. The agents buying art work for the czars seem to have understood that they needn't bother with anything religious or conscience-stirring. Still there is a profusion of astonishing treasures. The artists represented include da Vinci, Bruegel, Dürer, Holbein, Rembrandt, El Greco, Rubens, Van Gogh, Gauguin, Degas, Matisse, and Picasso.

A mile away, in the Russian Museum, none of the artists represented are "names" to the West, but a large part of the collection is both religious and conscience-stirring. Few of Leningrad's foreign visitors bother coming here, but I found it the more engaging museum, a sister to Moscow's Tretyakov Gallery. In both museums, it is thrilling to see the gradual discovery, especially by nineteenth-century Russian artists, of what is really Russian rather than lack-lustre imitation of western European painting. This parallels what was occurring in the writing of Pushkin, Dostoyevsky and Tolstoy. Together with the writers, the artists' attention encompassed both rich

51

and poor, the beautiful and the wretched. At least two of the painters, Ilya Repin and Nicholai Ghe, possessed a talent that can be compared to Rembrandt.

In a painting of the Last Supper, by Ghe, Judas is preparing to walk out while a deeply troubled Jesus stares at the floor. In Ilya Repin's painting of the raising of Jairas' daughter, Jesus looks like an intense young rabbi or Russian Orthodox priest as he stands over the dead child's body that he is about to summon back to life. In Vasili Polenov's painting of the woman caught in adultery, Jesus is marked mainly by the terrified gaze of the accused woman being pushed before him by a lynch mob. In these and similar paintings from the late 1800s, Jesus is not a remote and terrifying figure but a man among us living in a cruel world resembling our own.

Leningrad, February 20:

We were pilgrims today to the apartment where Dostoyevsky lived the last years of his life. The flat has been restored to something like the place it was when he was living there with his wife and their two children, while the adjacent rooms contain an exhibition about his life, including Russian and foreign editions of his books.

The icon — Our Lady of Sorrows — that was in his writing room has survived. Illumined by a vigil light, it hangs again in the corner of the room before the desk where he wrote *The Brothers Karamazov*. It was in this room that Dostoyevsky died January 28, 1881. We saw the note that his daughter wrote to him earlier that same day, "Daddy, I love you."

Over his wife Anna's writing desk there is a picture of the Nativity. "She was," Boris mentioned, "a deeply religious person with whom her husband often discussed religious questions." On her desk, in her own short-hand, were draft pages of *The Brothers Karamazov*. A much younger person, she survived her husband by nearly 40 years, living to see the Revolution.

In the adjacent exhibition, among papers and documents concerning his life and writing, we saw the kind of leg-irons he wore when he was a prisoner in Siberia. We also saw a photo of Fr. Amvrosy, the monk who so inspired him and who was a model for Fr. Zosima in *The Brothers Karamazov*. (I have heard the prediction that Fr. Amvrosy will be canonized during the Church's Millennium Celebration this year.)

We went on to the Peter and Paul Fortress, a walled island on the Neva and place of imprisonment and execution for many dissident Russians. In 1849, Dostoyevsky was about to be shot when the order from the czar arrived commuting his sentence to four years of hard labour and internal exile.

In the early evening Boris and I, after walking through heavy snow in a city park, went to the seminary for evening prayer. Boris pointed to an icon that had inspired a poem by Pushkin. Several students were lighting candles in front of it.

In the seminary chapel one is surrounded by choirs, a male choir to the right, a choir of mixed voices to the left, and in the balcony in back, a choir of women from the school's programme for choir directors.

It was the first time I have been in a church packed with young people. They were mainly students from other schools and institutes in Leningrad.

Leningrad, February 21:

Fr. Nicholas Preobrajensky, assistant rector of the seminary, has a prominent nose, short beard, a mass of hair on his head, and large, intense eyes. Aided by photos displayed in one corridor of the seminary, he told us the institution's history since its founding in 1809. The most surprising aspect had to do with the deep divisions within the Russian Orthodox Church at the time of the Revolution in 1917. In Leningrad, diverse factions took control of different parts of the seminary.

During much of the Stalin period, the seminary was closed, but in 1946 the seminary (no longer torn between factions) opened again. For a long time, only one hundred and fifty students were allowed, but in recent years there has been an enrolment of four hundred and fifty, at least a hundred graduating each year. Since 1978, seventy of the students in residence are women, a dramatic new turn for the Russian Orthodox Church. Mainly they are here to learn choral direction, but one woman is now working on a degree in theology. A three-storey women's residence fills much of what used to be the seminary's back yard. All the students wear black, though for the women a white lace bib is added. A number of couples met after the evening service. There are many student marriages following graduation.

As we sat in a language laboratory, having seen a student-made video film on the Orthodox Liturgy, I asked Fr. Nicholas to tell me about his background.

"Before coming to the seminary," he said, "I was a nuclear physicist. Had things gone a little differently in my life, I would probably be making nuclear weapons now!"

I asked him what had drawn him into physics. "I am attracted by exactness. I like things precise and punctual."

He laughed. "Perhaps that is why I am the one to make up the schedule for the seminary."

Born in 1944 in Pskov, he comes from a family of believers, which made his acceptance into a university physics programme exceptional, as this happened in the time of Khrushchev. Eventually he became an expert in the separation of isotopes. "Then I began to specialize in military applications at the institute where I was working. At this time I also had a few papers accepted for publication. I was married, a father. It was the beginning of success in my life, really, but I felt something was missing and was drawn toward the Church. In the Church I felt at home. Then I met Metropolitan Nikodim, at that time the head of the Church in Leningrad. He was a special person with a gift to encourage young people. He had an immense responsibility both here and in Moscow, yet sometimes he would spend thirty or forty minutes talking to me, even though the phone was ringing. My father and uncle also helped, bringing me books to read. Study is important. But I am the sort of person who has to look at everything through my heart. I like to feel and not only to know. Step by step, I turned toward another side. Then in 1978, after nine years in physics, I gave up my job at the institute and entered the seminary."

Wasn't it very hard to be given permission to leave nuclear physics? "Not at all. It was hard only for me to take the step. It was hard to change after so many years of work in a certain direction. But it became clear to me. I started giving my books to a colleague, perhaps to prepare him for the step I was about to take, showing him I didn't need these things anymore."

He graduated from the seminary after only three years, was ordained, assigned to a Leningrad parish, and then a few years ago was asked to return to the seminary as a member of the faculty. "I loved being in a parish and miss that. I like people and they like me and it was an unbelievable life. I still get letters from people in the parish. It was there more than in seminary that I discovered that I was born to be a priest, even though it was sometimes hard and exhausting. But I learned about the gospel in the parish, something you cannot learn in a classroom. Liturgical life is life itself.''

He has four children, a son and three daughters, ages five to fifteen. ''Every evening at bedtime I read them something about God. They like it. My son is reading the gospel and whatever he wants to ask, he asks, and I answer in front of all the children. Sometimes I organize a meeting with questions to discuss in front of the whole family. Sometimes they ask why in school do they say this or that and we talk about it. Perhaps one day they will be students here! But I don't want to push them.''

I asked if his father had tried to direct him into the Church. ''Never. He always said it was my decision — no one else could make it, and no one could force it. I agree. The Church doesn't need anyone who is pushed, only those who come from the heart. We need the passionate, we need energetic people, not those who are only luke-warm.''

As a young person, was he embarrassed to come from a family of believers? ''Yes. I tried to hide every trace of belief. I was ashamed to show it, to witness it, before students and teachers. If you wore a cross, they would say, 'Ah, so you're a priest!' It was a very hard time for believers. We didn't know what was coming. A lot of churches were closed. So I learned to give the answers they wanted to hear. You learn to say whatever is on television or in the papers. But now a new wind is blowing. It hasn't yet touched religion but we believe it will and we are beginning to live as if it had already touched us. This will be something new for all of us, this democratization.''

He mentioned as a particular example of the new climate the film, *Repentance*. ''It would never have been shown in earlier times. Now it is being shown all over the country and each theatre is filled. Our whole faculty went to see it together.''

Fr. Nicholas' sister died in the siege of Leningrad and his father — born 1915 — was in prison during part of the Stalin years, before the war. ''Yet my father never lost his Christian view. 'Receive life as it comes to you,' he always told us, 'and never hold anyone to blame but yourself.' Father knew those who had him arrested but he never spoke about them with anger.''

He returned to the discovery of his own vocation. ''In my childhood there were many pieces pointing toward the priesthood. Even the smell of incense — I remember that from childhood. I was away from the Church a long time but these memories helped me find my way back.''

It was a long conversation, much longer than either of us intended. Finally we embraced each other and said goodnight.

Sunday, February 22:

After waking to find fresh snow falling on the city, we returned to the seminary for the Holy Liturgy. It was more crowded than on weekdays, again mainly student-age participants but more older people. The singing was ravishing. The women's choir in the balcony invited me to stand with them. I went up just as people were lining up to receive communion and watched the slow simple ritual. I have never been in a Russian church where so many people were communicants on the same day, at least half the congregation. I wished I could be one of them. It is not only the ecclesiastical border that stands in the way but the preparation that Russians make for communion — much more than is presently required in the Catholic Church. "If you want to receive Communion," Boris explained, "you prepare in a hundred ways. On the evening before the Holy Liturgy, you go to the evening service and pray the canon of repentance. You pray to the Mother of God and the Archangel. You pray when you are waiting in line for a bus and in a store. You don't drink or eat after midnight. When you wake up you read the morning prayers. The night before or in the morning, you ask the priest to hear your confession."

We had lunch in the seminary refectory: soup, bread, whipped potatoes and a piece of boiled chicken. Nothing to drink and no dessert.

After lunch I talked with Fr. Alexander Ranne, Professor of Moral Theology. We had been together to the American Embassy in Moscow last week where he had described to the Embassy staff some of the discussions about war and peace going on in his classroom. He has a face shaped like an onion, a wispy beard and moustache, large and gracious eyes, a kind smile. He was born in 1952, has two children, a one-year-old son and a daughter, age seven.

His was no dramatic conversion story. "My father was a priest and I was grateful to be his son. I never felt like merging with the unbelievers. I sang in the choir and was a sub-deacon to Metropolitan Nikodim. I never had any hesitation with what side to take, although I did consider the invitation to join the Young Pioneers (similar to the Boy Scouts) when my teacher asked me. I came home and asked my father, 'Father, will you bless me to be a member of the Pioneers?' Father said to ask my teacher if I could wear both the Pioneer kerchief and the cross. The teacher said only the kerchief, so I didn't join. Everyone always knew that I was a believer. After the Army, I had a long discussion with my father and then entered the seminary."

He graduated in 1978, was married and ordained, then — his wife remaining in Russia — went to Rome for further study of moral theology. Apart from Christmas and summer holidays back in Russia, he was in Rome for three years, living at the Catholic Church's Russian College, the *Russicum*, while taking classes at the Gregorian Institute.

We talked about his teaching. "The topics in moral theology include marriage and celibacy, sexuality, teaching children how to live a moral life, relating to nature and technology, freedom, and vocation. It is a lot! I try to engage the students in dialogue. Sometimes I take a devil's advocate role to get them started. But usually they speak freely and easily."

I asked what is hardest to teach. "How to be patient! And questions about freedom — what it is and how to exercise it."

Boris and I walked out of the seminary to find the snow had stopped falling and the sky had cleared. Leningrad was sparkling again.

Each day in Leningrad we have tried to get into the Museum of Religion and Atheism in what used to be the Cathedral of Our Lady of Kazan. Surprisingly this prominent institution for the promotion of scientific atheism was closed each time we tried the door, but this afternoon it was open and we went in to look around.

"As a student," Boris recalled, "I used to come here and join a tour group and then correct the guide's mistakes. It was a little mischievous."

Boris found the museum had changed since his student days — no more graphic portrayals of the Inquisition or similar blood-stained horrors in Christianity's cellar, but a more subtle attack on religion. Note is even taken of some of the positive aspects of Christianity, especially the peace work Christians are engaged in. But the main message of both the displays and the guides is that, by and large, the Church has been indifferent to the poor if not actively exploiting them, that it frightens people with threats of hell and gets believers to put up with injustice in this world by the assurance of justice in heaven.

The museum had many visitors. We listened for a while to one of the guides, an attractive young woman fashionably dressed, explaining how the Church had cheated people out of money with the hope of miracles.

"It is clever to treat religion as something so dead that its relics, like dinosaur bones, need safekeeping in a museum," Boris said. "But I don't think it convinces many people."

The museum seemed to me infinitely sad, first of all because of the sins of Christianity down through the centuries are no fabrication, but still more because the museum locks rather than opens doors. It makes the churches look ridiculous and dishonest — easy enough to do — while ignoring or minimizing the positive aspects. The museum ignores the genuine questions that draw one toward God. The place strikes no spark of joy and communicates no sense of meaning.

Still there was some real beauty here. The exhibition that I found most engaging was a full-size model of a monk's hermitage — a rough-hewn log cabin with a narrow straw-covered plank for a bed, a simple table and chair, and an icon in the corner warmly lit by a vigil candle. Surely many visitors must find in this something beautiful and even challenging. It isn't an image of corruption but of people so drawn to God and so absorbed in prayer that they are absent-minded about the acquisitions and ambitions most of us consider so necessary.

61

The museum also exhibits many outstanding icons. I couldn't help but notice the reverence with which some visitors stood before these sacred images. "Even here," Boris remarked, "people take steps toward faith."

Novgorod, February 23:

Novgorod means New Town, which was true about eleven hundred years ago. The city is dense with ancient churches, seventy-seven of them, wonderful to look at though only a few of them are currently places of worship. In earlier times, when it was one of the principal cities of Russia, it was known as "Lord Novgorod the Great." Its circular kremlin, called the Detinets, stands on an embankment above the Volkhov River, with the Market Town on the facing bank. The present fortress wall of red brick was put up in the 1480s. In the centre is the Cathedral of St. Sophia, its six towers topped with green helmet-shaped cupolas.

We were welcomed to Novgorod by Fr. Michael, who has a very Russian face: pale skin, high forehead, hair combed straight back, the bone behind his eyebrows very pronounced, slate-blue eyes, huge hands, and mightily built, really, a body worthy of a bear. He was born in 1924 in Pskov. In 1944 he was badly wounded while fighting on the White Russian Front. After the war, he studied at the Leningrad Theological Seminary. He has been a priest nearly forty years, most of them in Novgorod. "It is a city," he said, "of churches, legends and saints." He is chairman of the city's Church Council and pastor of a local church, assisted by several priests and deacons.

He has a passionate spirit. "People don't just listen with their ears," he said over lunch, "but they feel with their heart. They know if Christ is in you or not."

We visited his own parish, the Church of Sts. Nicholas and Philip, part of which dates from the twelfth century. These were originally two adjacent churches facing different streets, but like an old married couple, they grew into each other. Now it is one structure, shining white, with shingled onion domes, wide log porches with rough wood stairs leading up to them, and two icons set into the outer walls of the church, with vigil candles flickering before them. On an icy day like this, as we trudged through deep snow, the icons were fireplaces of warmth and invitation.

Often the inside of an old church isn't as beautiful as the outside, but here the two are well matched, thanks to a new iconostasis made in the sixteenth-century style, the work of contemporary artists from Palekh. The dominating colours are mustard yellow, a thick creamy white, dark red, and dark green. There is no gold or silver overlay. The village of Palekh, north-east of Moscow, is internationally renowned for painting scenes from Russian legends and fairy tales on little boxes and brooches. Many of them are in museums. Before the Revolution, Palekh was a centre for painting icons. Some of the village artisans, having moved to Moscow, are reviving Palekh's earlier tradition.

There is a saint's body, Nikita of Novgorod, in the smaller church which is a place of prayer and veneration for many pilgrims. Fr. Michael lifted the coffin's glass lid so that Boris and I could kiss the silk vestment that covers the saint's face. This was a startling experience for me. In the Catholic Church, we also venerate not only the memory but the body of saints, but not this intimately. I managed to overcome my resistance. What a sweet fragrance arises from this ancient corpse! I shall never again regard the phrase, "the odour of sanctity," simply as a curious line of poetry.

We went back to St. Sophia's Cathedral. It was built between 1045 and 1050 when Prince Vladimir was still reigning in Kiev and Russian Christianity was in its infancy. It is a museum now, but Fr. Michael has arranged to have recordings of Orthodox chant played for visitors so that they can have a faint idea of what the place would be like as a living church.

Two of the cathedral's massive bronze doors also give witness to the undivided church that still existed when this building was put up. Brought here in the twelfth century from the city of Magdeberg, in northern Germany, then a trading partner of Novgorod, their surface is covered with reliefs of biblical scenes done in a fine Romanesque style, inscribed in both Latin and Slavonic. The doors mirror stone carving of the same period still found in numerous Romanesque churches in France.

It was intriguing to see in the back of the church a massive stone cross set within a circle, the Celtic rather than Russian or Latin types. This dates from the fourteenth century. Is it evidence that the Celtic monks came this far east, or that Novgorodian traders found their way to the Celts? Novgorod was a great trading city for centuries, doing business from Scandinavia to Constantinople. Were it not for the Russian carving on the face of the cross, and the Christ in the centre being crucified on the Orthodox six pointed cross, one would guess the cross had been brought here from the island of Iona in the Inner Hebrides or the mainland of Ireland.

In a nearby building is a museum with a remarkable exhibition of Novgorodian icons, though it contains but a fraction of its pre-war collection. Nearly all of the museum's five thousand icons were taken away during the Nazi occupation. Only five hundred have been recovered.

Some of the treasures of the collection were saved through the heroism of museum staff who entered the building despite heavy shelling of the town, taking what they could carry away to safe hiding places.

One of the rescued items is a sixteenth-century icon showing a miracle that occurred here in 1169 when the town was about to be attacked. The bishop had a dream in which he was told that he should bring a certain icon of the Virgin Mary from a nearby church and place it on the wall of the town. In the top third, one sees the icon, Our Lady of the Sign, being carried in procession into Novgorod, where some of the townspeople await it on their knees. In the middle section of the panel, the town under attack, the icon is mounted on the wall and is about to be struck by arrows fired by the enemy's archers. "One of the arrows struck the eye of the Virgin," Fr. Michael said, pointing out the wound in the icon. "Tears flowed from the icon, showering Archbishop John, who was standing underneath. It was a sign that the holy Virgin was begging God to spare our city." In the bottom section, the Novgorodian soldiers, three of whom are haloed as saints, ride out of the city gates with a sword-wielding angel flying overhead. Already some of the foe's horses are turned to flee. To the Novgorodians, the icon suggests that the city's real defence is Mary. For Fr. Michael she is still the defender not only of Novgorod but of Russia. Now this miracle-working icon is lodged in the museum. One can see where the arrow struck the eye-lid of Mary.

In the twelfth and thirteenth centuries, Novgorod, unlike most Russian cities, experienced a much greater mercy. It was spared the Tartar invasions. But Novgorod's good fortune ended in the fifteenth and sixteenth centuries. In 1456, and again in 1471, war broke out between Moscow and Novgorod. In both cases, Novgorod was defeated. Up to that time, Novgorod was a remarkably cosmopolitan principality run on democratic lines. Princes were elected and often deposed, and bishops too. A parliament — *veche* — was assembled for town meetings by the ringing of a great bell. When Ivan III subdued Novgorod the second time, he had the Veche Bell, symbol of the city's republican independence, removed. But, according to legend, the great bell tumbled off the cart not far from the city walls and shattered into many pieces. Each shard grew into a small version of the mother bell. "Ivan could take the bell and crush Novgorod's traditions," said Fr. Michael, "but he could not take from the people their longing to freely choose, and reject, their rulers." Small brass bells are still the city's main souvenir. I was given a set of three by Fr. Michael.

In 1570 Ivan the Terrible came to visit, an experience from which the city never fully recovered. Many leaders as well as common people of Novgorod were tortured to death or drowned in the river. In the Cathedral of St. Sophia, the ornate throne he occupied still stands.

All day Fr. Michael and our young guide, Tamara, took turns retelling the legends of Novgorod.

One story concerns a certain bishop of Novgorod who was

falsely accused of having an affair with a local woman. The bishop, deposed by the local people at a town meeting, was put on a little boat on the river, whose current normally would have carried him north to the next city. Instead the little boat went against the current toward a nearby monastery. Thus the people knew that the bishop had been chaste. The Novgorodians begged him to forgive them and remain. Perhaps the greater miracle is that, despite the calumny, he agreed to do so.

A curious fact about the River Volkhov is explained by a legend concerning a certain merchant of ancient times, Sadko, whose ship sank in a lake to the south. Under the water, he became acquainted with a mermaid princess who fell deeply in love with him and wanted to become his wife. But the prince missed his wife in Novgorod and longed for her so much that the compassionate princess gave him back his life in the mortal world. The princess was so saddened by his departure that her tears made the lake overflow its borders and form the river that now divides the city of Novgorod. The river, they say, is still made of her tears.

"This is why," said Fr. Michael, "our river is the only one in northern Russia that never freezes over." It is true that every other river we have crossed in the past week is frozen hard enough for trucks to drive across, while here the river is still flowing.

It is no legend that there are tears in this river. In the last war Novgorod was almost totally destroyed. A quarter million Russian soldiers, equal to the number of people who had lived in the city during the war, died in the battle to regain Novgorod. All but three of the city's churches were devastated during the war and have since been painstakingly rebuilt. The reconstruction is still going on nearly half-a-century later. One couple, now in their late sixties, have spent their entire working life reassembling the fragments of the frescoes of a certain church that was blown up as the German army withdrew. The walls have been rebuilt and now most of the frescoes are back in place. The couple hope to live long enough to complete their work.

67

We ate our evening meal by candle light in a small chamber, once a guard's room, high in the kremlin wall where a tower has been turned into a restaurant. The slit windows gave us a wondrous view of birch trees illumined by the sunset. We drank *kvas*, a mildly alcoholic drink made from black bread, and ate a big meal.

Fr. Michael asked what the Peace Forum in Moscow was like and what people in America and western Europe think about Gorbachev and the changes happening in the Soviet Union. I said the Forum would probably receive little press attention, but there was growing respect for Gorbachev and awareness that major change was going on.

Fr. Michael responded by recalling the writings of a second century theologian: "According the Church Father Tertullian, every soul is, of its original nature, Christian. This means that if you dig deeply enough, you will always find something of the image of God in each person. It's always there. I have seen this myself all my life. You find it in people who are certain that they are unbelievers, certain there is no God. This is how it is that our government stopped exploding nuclear weapons. The longing for peace is something deep in each person's soul. It is natural for the soul to want to live in peace, to do things for peace. In our church, all my life, I have always heard it taught that we must love everyone — believers, non-believers, Russian people, people from other countries. We are told to love people no matter what. Everyone is in your family. So it is natural to think about peace, and not only to think about it, but to think: What should I do? What is to be done? We are so capable, so strong. We make these big weapons. We are really clever. But are we clever enough to put them aside? Can we do something to make understanding? Can't we do that? Can't we do things that are good for life, things that don't destroy? Can't we do good and useful things?"

He paused, then added, "They say that Gorbachev's mother is a believer, and you know that babushkas have influence!"

I asked Fr. Michael if young people were becoming active

in local parishes. "Young people are mainly interested in football and hockey and pop music," he said. "Few of them have yet started thinking about the real questions of life. Still they are able to listen to you and to feel if Christ is in you. You have to speak to them heart to heart. When we do that, we find young people coming. Thanks be to God!" He made the sign of the cross as he said that. "I have a daughter, thirty years old. She and her family are believers. And they obey me."

He spoke of a six-year-old grandson who said, "Grandpa, when you sleep, your skin and body grows. How can it be that, without God, while I sleep, this happens?" Grandfather answered, "Everything, including your body, is made by God, and God made it to grow." This pleased my grandson. He is now coming to church and always holds out his hands in the Russian manner for me to give him a blessing. When he comes to stay the night in our house, he asks his grandmother at bedtime, "Babushka, will you read me prayers?"

Pskov, February 24:

Our train arrived in Pskov at three-thirty in the morning.
Despite the hour, two priests were awaiting us on the platform,
Fr. Constantine, huge and bearded, and Fr. Alexi, thin and
clean-shaven. Side by side they looked like the Russian version
of Laurel and Hardy. We were driven to the hotel in a car
with an icon over the rear-view mirror.

After four hours of sleep and then breakfast, we went to
Fr. Constantine's church, built in 1699 on the site of the oldest
Russian cathedral dedicated to the Holy Trinity. It stands
in the middle of the city's kremlin, towering over everything
else. In the upper church the iconostasis rises heaven-ward
like Jacob's Ladder. But, as it is winter, the upper church
was ice cold.

Fr. Constantine regards it as a miracle that the cathedral
survived the war. More than ninety per cent of Pskov's
buildings didn't, including most of the structures within the
kremlin walls. The German Occupation lasted three years,
involved many executions before the withdrawal, and ended
in general devastation. In a guide book I noticed grim photos
of some of the hangings that occurred in a public square near
the cathedral. As the Germans were getting ready to withdraw,
they placed explosives throughout the cathedral. At the cost
of their own lives, two Russian soldiers helped save the church.

In the lower church the morning service was in progress.
Over to one side, toward the back, was an open coffin
containing the body of an old woman. A funeral was set to
follow the Liturgy. Paying no attention to their dead
neighbour, the large congregation was matter-of-factly at
prayer around her.

Back in our car, we were on our way into the countryside.
The sky was a shining porcelain blue. We passed through a

70

succession of villages filled with old wooden houses. Dramatic icicles hung from the roofs. The wind constantly blew snow across the road. It seemed as if we weren't driving on the road but flying high above the ground over feathery cirrus clouds. The villages seemed nearly empty of people — it was too cold to come out except of necessity. The wooden houses were of many colours: bright blue, deep yellow, light brown, pink, dark red. Those few who braved the cold wore heavy fur hats and several coats. Occasionally we encountered pairs of horses pulling the kind of sleds Americans associate with Santa Claus. Mothers pulled sleds as well. Little bright-cheeked faces with large eyes were all that revealed the contents of the passive woolen bundles on the sleds.

"Here Russia begins!" So said Fr. Constantine as we passed through thousand-year old walls on a high hill behind the Church of St. Nicholas. We were about fifteen miles west of Pskov. We got out of the car and walked to an icy ledge on the steep hillside beyond the church. The walls we passed through weren't high but extremely thick, made of heavy unfinished stone. "These walls have withstood many enemies," Fr. Constantine said, patting the stone. The church within the walls, still a working church, is nearly as old as the walls, thus almost as old as Christianity in Russia.

From the hill we could see miles in every direction. There was a village below us, the bright colours of the houses emphasized by the snow, trails of smoke rising from the chimneys. On every side there were fields and forests and more hills. The immaculate scene looked as if it had been painted for us by a Russian Grant Wood.

Fr. Constantine is himself a sight to see: a face carved out of a football-size potato, flowing wild beard, thick eyebrows, greying hair combed straight back. I looked at him and thought, "*This* is where Russia begins!"

Our destination was the Pskovo-Pechorsky Monastery, on Russia's Estonian border, one of the principal centres of religious pilgrimage in the Russian Orthodox Church.

The monastery is built into a deep fold between two densely wooded hills. Nearly a mile of fortress wall is wrapped around this thicket of churches and other buildings. Before passing through the walls, Fr. Constantine took us along a path that makes a sudden turn and then offers a stunning view of the monastery. What a blaze of colour: gold, ultramarine, magenta, lemon, crimson, moss green, turquoise, and white snow. "Monks have lived here since 1400," said Fr. Constantine, "almost six centuries, and it has never been closed. Despite invasions, occupations, revolutions, it has been a place of uninterrupted prayer. It is one of our miracles. The walls have withstood nearly eight hundred assaults and siege after siege. It is Russia in miniature."

We turned back toward the monastery, passing under a candle-lit icon in the main gate, where we were met by one of the black-robed monks, Archimandrite Nathaniel. He has a long, deeply lined face, intense eyes, and a curly grey beard. This past Sunday, he mentioned, was the fortieth anniversary of his entrance into the monastic community. Before that, he was in the army. In fact, it being Armed Forces Day, he had pinned to his habit the two medals he won in the war. A number of the pilgrims at the monastery today were uniformed soldiers.

Fr. Nathaniel was quick to speak of Pskov's contribution to Russian history, and the monastery's contribution to Russian Orthodoxy: six canonized saints, many bishops, and two Patriarchs, including the Church's current head, Patriarch Pimen.

He led us into the monastery's caves where about ten thousand people are buried. Originally the caves were carved by water draining through the hills, but the monks have given them a uniform width and height and added linking passages where needed.

Entering the caves was a dream-like experience. Thin candles in hand, we stepped into the pitch black, narrow sandstone tunnels. The floor is covered with thick, fine sand. Fr. Nathaniel walked ahead of us, but *backwards*, so that he could more easily talk to us. He knows every inch and turn of the caves as a blind man knows the house he lives in so he had no need of a candle. The candles were for us. The one in his hand only served to illuminate his bearded face, which seemed to float in the dark before us.

We paused at many places to note markers in the wall. Occasionally we came upon small chapels. At one turn in the caves Fr. Nathaniel opened a low metal door. Inside we saw a large room carved into the rock with a coffin in the foreground draped in a black cloth embroidered in red that had been part of the robe of a monk who had recently died. Further back our candles faintly illumined similar coffins heaped high like boxes in a bin at the supermarket.

The remains of Pskov's saints are elsewhere in the caves in glass-topped coffins that can be opened for pilgrims, as two were for us. We reverenced the bodies, crossing ourselves and lightly kissing the vestments. One of them, St. Kornily, had been beheaded at the order of Ivan the Terrible. Just as in the little church in Novgorod, I discovered a remarkably sweet smell in the coffins.

Among the monastery's treasures are three "miracle" icons. One is an icon of the Dormition of Mary. The monastery is especially linked with the feast of Mary's passage into heaven, which it celebrates for three days in mid-August in the company of many thousands of pilgrims.

Fr. Nathaniel is an historian, theologian and poet. Again and again in our conversation he spoke of the importance of beauty. "The understanding of God," he said, "is the understanding of beauty. Beauty is at the heart of our monastic life. The life of prayer is a constant well of beauty. We have the beauty of music in the Holy Liturgy. The great beauty of monastic life is communal life in Christ. Living together in love, living without enmity, as peaceful with each other as one dead body is peaceful with another dead body. We are dead to enmity."

I was reminded of Dostoyevsky's words in *The Idiot*, "Beauty will save the world."

But Fr. Nathaniel has a sharp edge. He displayed a special irritation with atheists. "I say to them, 'You are not an atheist, you are a satanist. You know, just as Satan knows, that there is a God.'" So much for the Christian-Marxist dialogue at

Pskov! His fierceness fits him. He didn't become a monk to be a diplomat but rather to be free to be passionate about his faith.

I met a quite different personality in Fr. Zinon, the community's young but already famous icon painter. He did, for example, the iconostasis of the Church of the Protecting Veil at the Danilov monastery. I have heard people in Moscow compare Fr. Zinon with Rublev.

The community cherishes Fr. Zinon's vocation and has built an old-style log cabin as a place for him to work. A large window with glass assures him plenty of northern light. The room is warm not only from the stove but from the colours and the smell of paint. In one corner I noticed lapis lazuli stones being soaked in preparation for grinding. All the colours used to paint an icon are hand-made from natural substances, mostly minerals. On the easel was a part of the iconostasis he is painting for another church under restoration at the Danilov monastery, the Church of the Seven Ecumenical Councils.

I asked Fr. Zinon if he had been raised a believer. "No, though my mother is a believer. For me I started to come to belief when I was an art student. I was searching for some time for a copy of the Gospels and finally found a copy and then read them through. Then I decided." I was struck by the monastic directness of his answer. Though he is a young monk, thirty-three, he already has the simplicity I associate with the monastic life.

I asked him about icons. "They are not like civil painting. They aren't for museums. They aren't decorations. They are a reflection that God became man. They are holy doors."

Did he feel free to make changes in the traditional images? "The icon painter hasn't the right to change an icon just to be different. Icons carry the real feeling and teaching of Orthodoxy. It isn't the painter's own work. It is from heaven. We who are called to paint them are not icon producers. We never sign what we paint. We are just making copies."

Was special preparation needed to paint an icon? "Yes! It is the fulfilment of prayer. You need to feel the Spirit. You

74

can feel icons only during prayer. And icons are only for prayer. An icon is a place of prayer. You paint it in the same way you prepare for a church service, with prayer and fasting. It is a liturgical work. Preparing to paint an icon is like preparing to celebrate the Holy Liturgy."

We had both lunch and supper at the monastery. Lunch was in the refectory with all the monks, supper with the abbot, Fr. Gabriel, in a nearby house. The great treat on the abbot's table was pickled mushrooms that had been picked locally during the summer. "Come back someday with your wife and gather mushrooms," the abbot proposed. "Until you have picked mushrooms, you haven't been in Russia.

Pskov, February 25:

The day started with what was intended to be a brief stop at the Church of St. Nicholas and the Mother of God in a village adjacent to Pskov. A funeral was underway when we arrived. A coffin contained a babushka who seemed short and very thin. The family stood on one side of the coffin along with several ancient women, friends of the deceased. Each was holding a lit candle. The sons and daughters ranged from their thirties to their fifties. With them was a wide-eyed child of about four who watched everything with amazement. He reminded me of Yuri in the opening chapter of *Dr. Zhivago*. There was a choir of three. The priest, Fr. Vladimir Popov, incensed the body, sang prayers, put a paper and candle in the hands of the dead woman, then each friend and relative kissed her hands and forehead. The daughters and old women wept, the men looked as if they were carved from stone, the child seemed deeply puzzled. A cotton burial shroud was laid over the body while the choir sang, "Dust thou art and to dust thou shalt return, until the day of the resurrection." An icon of the Resurrection was on a stand in the middle of the church. The coffin lid was laid over the body and with solid blows the nails were hammered in, a terrifying sound that announced death more vividly than any words.

After the funeral, Fr. Vladimir invited us to have a cup of tea with him at his home, a small wooden house nearby. His wife, though a medical doctor employed at the clinic of a local factory, happened to be home and insisted we have something to eat. While she went into the kitchen, Fr. Vladimir showed us the icon corner of their living room. One of the pictures was of a saint recently canonized by Pope John Paul II: Maximillian Kolbe, a Polish Catholic priest who, while a prisoner at Auschwitz, gave his life to save a Jewish inmate. In the picture Kolbe is shown as an emaciated man in striped prison uniform.

We were called to the kitchen table for a meal of *blini*, mushrooms, melted butter, pickled fish, beets and sweet nuts, plus vodka and tea.

"It isn't possible to know the Orthodox Church from outside," Fr. Vladimir said. "It is mostly hidden. It is in the house as much as it is in the church. There are so many special rituals for each hour, each season. This week, the week before Lent, we eat *blini*. It is a life full of meaning and inspiration. And it always seems original!"

Fr. Vladimir's wife, Helen, showed me a photograph of their son, nineteen years old, now in military service in the far east on Kamchatka Peninsula. Despite his uniform, he looked so young.

A priest's wife is often addressed as *matushka* (mother). I asked her if it was hard being a *matushka*. "In some ways, yes, and yet again, no. It is a vocation and it can only be done if you are willing to love. You have to be a spiritual person, a praying person."

I asked how they met. "It is a wonderful story," Fr. Vladimir answered. "It is really amazing. Helen's father was a priest in Siberia, in Tomsk, and I visited him. I was doing my military service. He showed me his daughter's photograph and I said immediately, 'That's my wife!' When Helen and I actually met we loved each other from the beginning and now it is more than twenty years we are together. Our marriage was, I think, something that happened to us even before we met."

I asked about changes he had witnessed in his thirteen years as priest of the local church. "Many changes. At that time our church was in very bad condition. Everything had to be repaired. But it wasn't only the building that was in trouble. We have had to repair the congregation as well. But now it is quite a happy church. We really care for each another. We have a choir of twenty. Even those people who rarely come, like the children of the woman we buried today, are glad we are here. And we have more and more young people coming.

In the last ten years the average age has gone down from the fifties to the forties, and some are only in their teens and twenties. There is a higher level of education among believers. There is *perestroika* [reconstruction] going on in the political sphere of this country, but it has been going on even longer in the Orthodox Church. The outside *perestroika* begins with inner *perestroika*. The spiritual life is the inside of the social life.''

We said goodbye reluctantly, then drove deep into the countryside to the estate of Mikhailovskoye. Here the poet and writer Alexander Pushkin lived during two crucial years of his internal exile, from 1824 to 1826, when he was punished for his involvement with revolutionary discussion groups. He was twenty-five when ordered to leave St. Petersburg.

For two centuries Pushkin has been part of the glue holding Russians together. Often Russians recite his poetry by heart. His poems and stories are the basis of ballets and operas. His statue seems to be in every park. Wherever he lived there is a museum in his memory. Mikhailovskoye is a place of pilgrimage.

Fr. Gabriel, abbot of the Pskovo-Pechorsky Monastery, and one other monk met us there. The abbot knows the museum director, Simeon Geichenko, and had arranged for us to meet him. He and his wife live in a house close to the one Pushkin occupied, offering a similar view of the Sorot River, now solid ice, and beyond it miles and miles of unspoiled hills and forests. To honour Pushkin, the region is closed to industry. Practically speaking, the view we saw is the same view that refreshed Pushkin's eyes on a winter day.

We entered the director's home through a large enclosed porch sheltering an extensive collection of samovars, the traditional Russian device for providing a ready supply of boiling water so that tea can be brewed at any moment. While all samovars are fashioned on the same principle — a reservoir for water built around a column containing hot coals — the design possibilities are as diverse as the variations in Russian church architecture. There were several hundred samovars on this porch, no two quite the same. In addition one wall was covered with horseshoes, a long row of small bells hung from a ledge over a window, and the ceiling was plastered with strips of bright coloured paper. The intense smell of warm cinnamon enveloped us the moment we entered the house. I felt like I was falling through the rabbit hole in *Alice's Adventures in Wonderland*.

We passed into the kitchen, the source of the cinnamon smell, then through a narrow hallway into Simeon Geichenko's study. Apart from the window over his desk, the room was lined with books floor to ceiling, with an island of additional bookcases standing in the middle. A narrow bed covered with a patchwork quilt stood in a back corner. Pushkin's death mask was on the wall as well as several of Pushkin's drawings.

Simeon Geichenko is now eighty-seven. Before the war, he was director here, then he fought in defence of Leningrad. The war cost him his left hand. Ever since he has been back here running the museum, organizing Pushkin conferences, and writing books and essays.

Fr. Gabriel brought a new book for the director's library, a *samizdat* (self-published, unofficial) essay about Pushkin. Fr. Gabriel said the author lives in Leningrad. "*Saint* Leningrad," the director responded. (Leningrad was originally named St. Petersburg.)

We went to Pushkin's small, unpretentious house. Icons hang in a corner of each room, clean embroidered linen draped over the tops, sprigs of herbs tucked behind the frames, and fresh flowers in vases beneath the vigil candles. "In this house Pushkin turned toward Russian rather than European sources of inspiration," Boris said. "His nanny, Arina Rodionovna Yakovleva, was a woman of deep faith and love of Russia. While most of the intellectuals in St. Petersburg were speaking French better than Russian, she opened the door into Russia for Pushkin. He loved to hear her retell the traditional Russian stories and later he made some of them into poems that today every Russian child knows by heart."

Boris recited part of a poem written by Pushkin later in his life, after his nanny's death:

Here is the house of my disgrace
Where with my nurse for company I lived.
She is no more, no more I'm hearing
In the adjacent room her heavy paces,
The patient way she goes upon her rounds . . . [3]

As in so many cities, there is a statue of Pushkin in Pskov, but in Pskov's case his nanny is shown sitting behind him, knitting, as if to say, no Arina Rodionovna Yakovleva, no Pushkin. In the icons and spinning wheel at Mikhailovskoye, one senses her abiding presence.

In 1837 Pushkin was buried, as he had wished, at the Svyatogorsky Monastery not far from Mikhailovskoye. The church is at the top of a steep hill with Pushkin's grave just behind the church. I remarked what a pity it was that the monks were gone and the place now only a museum. Fr. Gabriel said it was his hope that he would live to see a monastic community here again. "Pushkin didn't want to be buried in a museum but in a place of prayer."

We had a meal together at a local restaurant. Late in the meal Fr. Gabriel fixed me in his stone-steady gaze and said, "We need the Holy Spirit's influence! With the Holy Spirit, we can solve every problem. Whatever action is inspired by the Holy Spirit is more important than any speech or any project. What we need is the Holy Spirit! Everything else comes afterward."

He toasted the book I am writing. "What you see of our country, our church, our people, how we live, what is good, what is not good — all these things you have to tell. Tell what you have seen and how you have felt. It is a missionary work. You are making a bridge between believers East and West and also between believers and non-believers. May the Holy Spirit give you strength and understanding. May God help you in your good actions!"

He prayed the book would be a contribution to peace. "King David said that for God a thousand years are like a single day. But time is very important to us! If God gives us a day, he

3. Simon Geichenko, *Alexander Pushkin Museum Park* (Moscow: Planeta Publishers, 1982); poem translated by Peter Tempest.

gives us a thousand years. So much depends on what we do with the time God gives us. If we live in love, God may give us an extra day, an extra thousand years. What does it mean to God to give us a thousand years? Nothing! But it is important for us. And these days, these years, they are not just for you and me, not just for believers, but for everyone, for the whole world.''

He pointed out that his friend, Simeon Geichenko, is a member of the Communist Party and therefore presumably a non-believer, though, as I am so often reminded, one never really knows who believes and who doesn't. But Simeon Geichenko, said Fr. Gabriel, "is a good man for believers. He is always eager to welcome whomever I send to him." Fr. Gabriel recalled that when he was first elected abbot, he was only thirty-five, and Simeon Geichenko used to say to him, "How is it going, sonny?" But now when he sees the abbot he says, "How is it going, granddad?"

Moscow, February 27:

After an night ride on the train from Pskov, we arrived at six-thirty in the morning. A theological student was waiting for us and took us to the Hotel Ukraina. After a nap, I woke to find Moscow under a clear sky of pale colours. There was less snow than there was two weeks ago.

The apartment building across the street is crowned by a red and white sign a hundred yards wide: "Yes to the peaceful policies of the Leninist state!" The same banner was there in 1983 and there are similar ones in prominent places in Soviet city and town. But I have never noticed Russians looking at them. I remember an Intourist guide who said, "We no longer see these signs. They are mainly to alarm tourists."

I discovered I had left my one good pair of trousers in Pskov. Nothing had been ironed for two weeks. I occasionally managed to do laundry in the bathroom sink but my jacket and trousers were looking as if they had been run over by a parade of trucks.

Boris's solution was to take me clothes shopping at the GUM department story on Red Square. It is an amazing place: a vast, glass-roofed green-house three tiers high, full of shops, cut through with pedestrian avenues and laced with overhead wrought-iron bridges that give a stunning view of this pre-revolutionary palace of commerce and cash registers. In the very centre is a large fountain.

I bought a three-piece grey suit, good enough for a banker but with buttons where American clothing would have zippers, and also a pair of pyjamas for future train rides.

After wandering around GUM we walked the neighboring streets until our feet were numb from the cold, then went back to the hotel where I put on the suit. After two weeks in the same woollen jacket, it was a major transformation. I was no longer the scruffiest American in the USSR. After lunch, we went out to the Danilov Monastery where I visited the Church of the Protecting Veil to pray and have another look at the iconostasis painted by Fr. Zinon.

We stopped to see Archdeacon Vladimir Nazarkin, on the staff of the Church's External Affairs Department, who had spent the morning at a meeting of the Commission preparing the Millennium celebration. We had met several times, but I have one special memory of him: I was sitting next to him one night on my first visit to Moscow when I tried to keep up drop for drop with the Russians and ended up hardly able to walk. Vladimir consoled me by recalling that I was lucid until the very end. We drank tea this time.

Boris is suddenly gone. His brother arrived unexpectedly in Moscow today. We had a hurried goodbye and embraced each other with emotion. For the next few days I'll be with Georgi Dereviantchenko, who had arranged for Boris and me to travel together.

I went for a long solitary walk in Gorky Park, enjoying the crunch of snow and the sight of a few couples wandering the park paths.

Zagorsk, February 28:

Georgi was at the hotel in time for breakfast, and with him was a colleague, Tatiana Tchernikova. It was Tatiana who first took me to a living Orthodox church three years ago and taught me how to bow, how to cross myself, and how to stand — never to put my arms behind my back or in my pockets.

Driving north to the Holy Trinity-St. Sergius Lavra in Zagorsk, I asked them about the Russian Orthodox way of keeping Lent. "We keep a strict Lent," Georgi said. "No meat, no milk, no butter, no cheese, no eggs. But we don't starve to death. We eat potatoes, bread, and vegetables — salted cucumbers, tomatoes, mushrooms — and we drink a lot of *kvas*. Also there are three days of exception: the Annunciation, the Feast of the Forty Martyrs, and Palm Sunday."

I asked about Georgi's background. "We have the saying, 'When trouble comes, open the gates wide.' Everyone in the Ukraine, everyone in Russia, knows how true it is. My father died in combat two weeks after the German invasion. My mother and two brothers and sister and I spent the next three years living under German occupation in the Ukraine."

I asked how much he remembered of the war. "I was only seven when it started, but I remember everything. Everything! We children had to work and work hard. In the towns and cities, eighty per cent of the adult population around us were women, in the villages ninety per cent. Children worked side by side with their grandparents. We grew quicker than children should grow, but not in size. We became older than our age. There wasn't enough food. Living under the Occupation, we saw horrible things. People were hung, people were shot. You would see the bodies hanging there. I

84

remember the hanging of a woman whose husband was a partisan — she had come into the town, more than eight months pregnant. She was hung with her unborn child and the body left hanging in the middle of town, the word *partisan* attached to her dress over her belly. The mother and child were left there to rot. It was in 1943. Until now I remember it. I can never get this out of my thoughts.

"And the most horrible thing was that you got used to these crimes! They became normal life. It is hard for our children to understand why we older people are the way we are — why we take nothing for granted, why we can't stand to see anything wasted. Sometimes we are angry with our children who have never known anything like that and can't imagine what it was like and what we went through.

"It is amazing what children can survive. It was much harder for my mother, going through the war without her husband, and with four children depending on her. It wrecked her health, but she survived and lived until 1968."

Georgi got a law degree before going into the Moscow Theological Seminary in Zagorsk, but when he graduated in 1958, no one in the class was ordained. It was during that period of renewed religious repression under Khrushchev when thousands of churches were closed. "In some ways it was a terrible time, but in other ways not. I try to remember the good. Now Metropolitan Pitirim proposes that the Church ordain me, but I hesitate. It would require such a re-organization of my life. I think I am too old for such changes."

Georgi is a friend of Fr. Gabriel, the abbot of the Pskovo-Pechorsky Monastery. They were both in Jerusalem and spent a great deal of time together. Both Fr. Gabriel's parents were killed in the war. He was raised by a priest.

As we reached the last hilltop before Zagorsk and saw all those glorious churches and towers in the distance, I asked where the pilgrims stay. On the great feast days many thousands come, but pilgrims are plentiful every day of the year.

"There are hotels," Tanya answered. "Or do you mean *real* pilgrims? The real pilgrims won't stay in hotels. They have walked here, some of them walking for many weeks, and they sleep wherever they can, under bushes, in the houses of those who offer them a bed, in sheds, whatever they can find. In Zagorsk they sleep inside the monastery walls.''

So there are still real pilgrims in Russia, the holy tramps, the fools for Christ. Old Russia, Holy Mother Russia, is still quietly, stubbornly existing after all these years.

In fact most of the people coming here, though they come by bus or train or car, are also pilgrims, even if living a settled life with a normal job and no chance for thousand-mile walks. I saw the devout attitude in their faces as they passed under the main gate leading through the walls into the monastery ground. They are coming to stand and pray in a holy place.

But, as I noticed during the time we lived in Jerusalem, there are also many tourists, people who come because they have heard it is something special, something beautiful and amazing, something historic, and of course it *is* amazing, this flock of colourful churches behind these massive walls.

It was a blessing to be there, to again venerate the body of St. Sergius, and to stand quietly before the Trinity icon.

We met Fr. Vladimir, the seminary's assistant rector, an archpriest, forty-seven years old, father of two children. Over lunch we talked about bread. I told him about Rosemary Lynch, a Franciscan sister who is seventy years old, and lives in Las Vegas, Nevada, where she helps receive refugees. One of those put in the care of her community was a Russian whose profession is the restoration of icons, unfortunately a skill with no employment possibilities in Nevada. All that the nuns could find for her was a job clearing tables in a casino restaurant. Because of a state law requiring that food left on the table be thrown out, the work provoked a crisis of conscience for the woman. She was horrified having to throw away uneaten food, but especially bread. She came home one night in tears, saying, ''They make me throw away the body of Christ!'' She finally quit the job.[4].

4. Jim Forest, ''A Franciscan in the Nuclear Desert,'' an interview with Sr. Rosemary Lynch, O.F.M., *Reconciliation International* 2, no. 5 (November 1987) 8-11.

The Vice Rector nodded his head as he listened. "I can understand her. If we drop a piece of bread on the floor, we pick it up, kiss it, and eat it. We cannot imagine throwing bread away. This has always been true for us, but since the last war, we also think of all the people who starved. Even though bread costs almost nothing to buy, it contains a lot of work. All bread is holy. All bread is a reminder of the Saviour."

We talked about exiles, their loneliness, the disappointments they often experience, their nostalgia and bitterness. Yet some manage to build bridges between Russia and the West. He mentioned as an example Nicholas Zhernov, whose book, *The Russians and their Church*, I have been reading.

On the way back to Moscow, Georgi continued the conversation about those who seek exile and those for whom exile would be the worst punishment. "We usually have an attitude of loyalty toward our country even if we don't agree with the leaders. Motherland is motherland! It is our mother and many of us can't understand how anyone would leave or even want to leave. Often there are hard feelings about such people. But still they are our brothers, our sisters. Sometimes we know some of them personally. Anyway, it is never simple. Every family has troubles, every group has troubles, every society, every country has troubles — every *one* has troubles! One of the best ways to forget about your own troubles is to be an expert on the troubles of someone else, to condemn that other person instead of facing your own guilt. But we Russians say, 'Don't trouble trouble until trouble troubles you.' "

After supper in the hotel I ran into Tamara, who is employed by the Russian Orthodox church. She was with her husband. "Be careful," she said, "this man is a member of the Communist Party. But what can I do, he is also my husband and he has a few good points." They invited me to eat some apples and share a bottle of champagne. "She is a believer and I am not, so we are enemies," her husband said with a smile. I asked him how it was living with a believer. "Terrible! She gets up in the morning and instead of making breakfast, she stands in front of the icons and prays!'' ''But do you know what I am praying for?'' she said. ''I am praying that you will learn to cook breakfast.''

Vladimir and Suzdal, March 1:

After a long ride east from Moscow on roads clogged with trucks, Fr. Germann welcomed Georgi and me to Vladimir. Fr. Germann is a monk, thirty years old, tall, with long hair, a full beard, fine features, a piercing gaze. Fr. Germann radiates both joy and rootedness. Wearing his black velvet monk's cap and long black coat with black fur collar, no one overlooks him when he passes by. I enjoyed watching people staring at him as he sailed down the street.

Fr. Germann's nature is "at all times and everywhere to give thanks to Almighty God." While we were in Vladimir's Dormition Cathedral, I mentioned to him that this church must have wonderful acoustics. Though we were far from alone in the cathedral, he immediately sang an exuberant "Amen" — long, unrestrained, banner-like. The whole huge church vibrated in an astonishing way.

The Dormition Cathedral, for centuries the home of the Vladimir icon of the Mother of God, was built in 1189, replacing a smaller church that had been destroyed by fire. In 1238 the cathedral was the scene of tragedy: the Tartars, having broken through the city ramparts, attacked the cathedral, burning all who had sought refuge within its walls: the prince and his family, the bishop and crowds of towns people. It was the first of many Tartar assaults on Vladimir. Even so most of the church survived, including parts of a fresco of the Last Judgment.

Adding to the cathedral's beauty are several frescoes by Andrei Rublev painted in 1408. In one of these, St. Paul is preaching to a crowd, an exhorting arm raised in the air, his other hand gesturing towards the Kingdom of God, very much the model for many twentieth-century paintings of Lenin.

89

Russian revolutionary iconography has its roots in Russian religious iconography.

The Holy Liturgy is celebrated here daily, as well as other offices of prayer, plus funerals and baptisms. It is a busy, lively church served by five priests, five deacons, and at least one nun. Two choirs take full advantage of the church's acoustics.

We looked at several other churches and visited a museum with a local guide who knew dates and names and historical terms but who revealed little of the spiritual meaning of what we saw. Fr. Germann added what was missing. I noted the guide was as fascinated as I was.

We drove thirty miles to Suzdal, a smaller town but crowded with beautiful churches, though only one of them a living parish. "In Suzdal," Georgi noted, "you see ancient Russia. The first Russian settlers came here in the eleventh century. From the sixteenth century to the twentieth century, very little changed. No trains or factories ever came here. Ever since the Revolution, it has been forbidden to build any new structures. An exception was made for the hotel where we are staying, but it had to be put out of sight. People consider Suzdal the most beautiful town in Russia."

The Convent of the Intercession was once the dwelling place for women belonging to the nobility, including the dismissed wives of Ivan the Terrible and Peter the Great. The nuns are gone and their refectory now is a restaurant where we had an exceptional meal, yet I could hardly pay attention to it as I was so absorbed in listening to Fr. Germann.

We found a special bridge between us in St. Seraphim of Sarov, whose compassionate face appears in icons in every living church. St. Seraphim, though he died only one hundred and fifty years ago, has become one of the most beloved saints in the Russian Orthodox Church. "St. Seraphim helped me to become a believer," said Fr. Germann. He has in his care a fragment of the rock on which St. Seraphim prayed for a thousand days. It was a gift from an old nun who knew a nun who knew a nun who knew Seraphim. The saint's few possessions, among them the heavy cross he wore, were in the custody of the convent that formed near him at Diveyevo.

"St. Seraphim is a unique saint," said Fr. Germann. "With St. Sergius, I think he is the most beloved saint in the Russian Church. Believers venerate him wholeheartedly. In him and his character, in his spirituality, we find the principle Christian characteristics — love for all people without exception, and a readiness to sacrifice. That's why people love him so much."

"We live in a time that pays special homage to advanced education and intellectual brilliance," Fr. Germann added. "But faith isn't just for the clever. Though he prepared for a career in architecture, Seraphim didn't graduate either from university or seminary. All his ideals were gifts from God revealed through prayer and deeds. And so through St. Seraphim many different people are drawn to belief — the intellectuals, the simple, and now not only people in the Russian Orthodox Church but other churches."

He told me a very Russian tale about a rich man who came to St. Seraphim and was healed by him, so healed that the man gave up all his wealth and embraced holy poverty. The man, Mikhail Mondarov, had a young sister, age twenty-eight, who joined the community of nuns associated with Seraphim. When her brother was dying, she wanted to die in his place, though, as she confessed to St. Seraphim, she was terrified of death. "Please bless me father. I'm afraid to die." Seraphim responded: "Why be afraid? For us death opens the way to eternal joy." After she left him, she fell ill and died, but her brother lived on for many years. She is buried near the monastery. Fr. Germann, who sometimes goes to Sarov, has visited her grave.

Before his death, St. Seraphim said to the sisters: "My joys, come as often as you can to my grave. Come to me as if I'm alive and tell me everything, and I will always help you."

Because of St. Seraphim, Sarov is a place of pilgrimage. Though no working church is presently functioning there, two elderly nuns receive pilgrims and pray with them, showing the relics handed down to them, occasionally giving a fragment away as they did to Fr. Germann. "St. Seraphim *is* the face of the Church," said Fr. Germann.

We talked about the monastic life, which has never been

easy to understand for those outside it, and which is almost incomprehensible in the modern world. "In our society," said Fr. Germann, "the monk's vocation is very strange. Not everyone can understand it and certainly it isn't for everyone, in fact it is for very few. Yet there are still many who feel drawn to it, who want to have the fullest possible spiritual life and to withdraw as much as possible from civil life." This withdrawal is complicated by the dearth of monasteries and convents. "But the way opens if you are patient. We live singly or in pairs in small apartments and spend most of the day either in the church or visiting the sick or tending to other needs. At home we live the monastic life much as it would be lived in community."

I asked what occasioned his religious awakening. "It was something natural but it is hard to describe. I was eighteen when it began. To learn about the church, not knowing anyone to tell me, I borrowed atheist books from the library and often could find in them parts, quotations, for example, that helped me, though the books themselves weren't very deep. Atheism can't really influence anyone. It can't answer the deepest questions. It can't give a direction in life. But when you read about a saint like Seraphim, even if you aren't a believer, you can't help but be impressed. After some time I felt led to go to the Holy Trinity Lavra in Zagorsk and there I had the idea that before I died, maybe I would be a monk. And now I am already five years a monk, and only thirty! Thanks be to God! In families of non-believers, believers often emerge. Young people go to church. They become believers, priests, nuns and monks. Sometimes they lead their parents to belief. The monk in front of you is such a person! Now my mother is a believer, and my sister sings in the cathedral choir."

We talked a little about the Russian Orthodox Church. "It is both conservative and demanding, reluctant to accept any change and cautious about new ideas. Throughout the year we have a long Liturgy, even in winter. But this aspect has protected our Liturgy. Orthodox people don't want changes that would make it quicker or less demanding. We want to be servants of God. This is our freedom. That is what it means to us to be believers. Yet many miracles come from such living. You develop a deep sense of gratitude and awe. The beauty of our services cannot be appreciated in a hurry. But when you have time, the singing becomes the highest prayer. Our prayers are poetry and they have to be sung, and the authors, like St. John of Damascus, are the finest poets.''

There are various ways of understanding history. For Fr. Germann, for whom the central reality is God, human history is the history of the saints, a saint being anyone for whom God is at the centre of life. ''Each saint is a unique event,'' said Fr. Germann, ''a victory over the force of evil. So many blessings can pour from God into the world through one life. And such holiness is so needed in these times when there are so many who are poor in faith, when so many aren't fond of the spiritual life or the Christian faith. Let the Lord give us more saints.'' Saying this, and with a cheerful smile, he crossed himself.

Before parting, Fr. Germann taught me a short prayer in Russian, ''*Bozhe milostiv budi mi greshnomu*'' — Lord, be merciful to me a sinner. ''Use it while you are flying back to Holland tomorrow.''

APRIL 1987

Before leaving Moscow at the beginning of March, an invitation came for me to return at Easter. "Easter for the Orthodox is what Christmas is for the churches in the West," said Metropolitan Fileret of Minsk. "It is our season of complete joy. You cannot write about our Church and not describe how we celebrate the Resurrection."

Moscow, Holy Thursday, April 16, 1987:

Vladimir Tyschuk met me at the airport. "Call me Volodya," he said. "Metropolitan Fileret has asked me to help you in your travels for the next two weeks." He is twenty-three years old, plump, has a pink, round face, ruddy blond hair, a young moustache, wears a black leather jacket, works for the Church's External Affairs Department, and hopes soon to begin theological studies. "I am following our family tradition," he explained. "My father is a priest. Until recently he was pastor of a church in the north of Moscow. Now he is pastor of a Russian Orthodox parish in Tokyo."

I complimented him on his English. "It's easy for me. When I was twelve and thirteen, with my mother and sister, we lived in New York, where father was one of the priests serving at the Russian Orthodox Cathedral on East 97th Street."

After checking me into the Ukraina Hotel, we decided to see the icon collection at the Andrei Rublev Museum, in earlier times the Andronikov Monastery, a place Volodya often visits.

There are sometimes significant differences between icons bearing the same name and involving the same composition. While there is only one original of the Vladimir icon of the Mother of God, for example, there are hundreds of thousands that are closely modelled on it and which bear the same name.

Moving slowly through the exhibition, I found myself attentive to little things in icons I hardly noticed six months ago — tiny differences in colour, aspects of expression, the gestures of hands and eyes. So much of the art of the icon is nuance.

In the basic elements of composition, the artist simply does what others did before, working within guidelines that go back to the Russian Church's Council of One Hundred Chapters six hundred years ago and, before that, to the Seventh Ecumenical Council in 787. At both Councils it was taken for granted that an icon is primarily a work of spirituality. The icon painter, the Russian Council ruled, must be "meek, mild, pious, not given to idle talk or to laughter, not quarrelsome or envious, not a thief or a murderer."[1] Nothing is said about artistic ability, but of course that was necessary too and often was of a very high order. "The best icons are the work of skilled masters," Volodya pointed out, "yet it is not always the most competent who touch my heart most deeply."

It is really a mystery why a particular icon throws open a door within the soul and makes it easier to experience God's presence. There is a superficial similarity between Rublev's icon of the Holy Trinity and many copies by later masters, yet it is rare to discover one that communicates a similar spirit. The angelic faces and bodies often seem rigid, with eyes more suggestive of judgment than love.

We saw a fifteenth century icon of John the Baptist by Rublev or one of his students. The Baptist is often portrayed as being fierce, but here he is imploring God's mercy on behalf of all sinners, and no one could be less ferocious. The painter used few lines, the detail is minimal. The eyes are shaped in a maternal way that mirrors the eyes of the divine figures in the Trinity icon.

I stopped for a long time in front of two sixteenth century icons that formerly were in the Assumption Cathedral of the Kyrill-Belozershy (Kyrill-White Lake) Monastery two hundred miles from Moscow. In the first Jesus' body is being taken down from the cross, in the next the disciples are burying him. In both icons Mary's face is pressed against the face of her son. It is the same action, the same relationship of faces, as in the Vladimir icon of the child Jesus and his mother, except the roles are reversed. In the Vladimir icon, Jesus is pressing *his* face against Mary's in a gesture of consolation

1. M.V. Alpatov, *Early Russian Icon Painting* (Moscow: Iskusstvo Press, 1978), p. 23.

as she gazes into a future that leads to the cross. Now it is Mary pressing her face against her son's at the foot of the cross when all that she had dreaded has finally happened.

Another icon, painted in Moscow in the late sixteenth century, is of Anne and Joachim, the parents of Mary, embracing each other. They seem so connected, so deeply in love. I don't recall ever seeing in western religious painting such a celebration of marriage. At least since the division of the Western and Eastern Churches in the eleventh century, it is rare for those canonized in Rome to be married, which perhaps helps explain why the Catholic Church has the tradition of clerical celibacy, links holiness with celibacy, and is better known for sexual prohibitions than sexual affirmation. This icon suggests that to love someone in marriage is to participate fully and intimately in God's love for that person. It is from such a depth of love that Mary was born.

In a new building on the monastery grounds there is an exhibition of skilful copies of frescoes by Rublev and other masters. I was most surprised by a wonderful fresco of Christ in glory by Rublev — Christ looking like a smiling dancer. Over and over again in Rublev's work, there is a stunning and joyous sense of God's love, that depth of mystical encounter that Thomas Merton referred to as "mercy within mercy within mercy."

In the middle of the monastery stands one of the most beautiful structures in Moscow, the Spassky (Saviour) Cathedral: small, exquisite, light as air. Built in 1420, it was very badly damaged but it is now restored on the outside.

A bronze statue of Rublev stands in the small park outside the monastery's main gate. Rublev is shown as a tall lean figure in a simple monk's habit, an inward gaze in his eyes, his hands supporting wood panels that rest at his feet. It is exceptional work with an icon's epic calm. "There is a rumour that Rublev will be one of those canonized at the Church Council next June," Volodya told me.

In order to keep Lent, we ate in a little cafe rather than in the hotel restaurant. We had a meal of bread, cucumbers, and raspberry soda.

98

Afterward, with Volodya away to take care of travel arrangements, I had a long walk with a retired English pastor visiting Moscow as part of a Pax Christi group. We strolled southward on Kalanin Prospekt, away from the Kremlin, stopping in a sidewalk cafe for a raisin-bread bun and a glass of apple juice with slivers of apple at the bottom of the glass, all for seventeen kopecks.

Moscow, Good Friday, April 17, 1987:

This morning we met with the Dean of the Church of Our Lady, Joy of the Sorrowful, Fr. Boris Guznyakov, a tall man with a grey beard and a deep scar on one cheek. He has been worshipping in this central-Moscow church for forty years, since the parish was re-opened after being restored from damage it suffered in the war. He has been a priest here for twenty-six years. He reads Shakespeare and treasures an edition of the Authorized Translation of the Bible printed in Oxford in the nineteenth century.

I asked him if the congregation had changed greatly in the forty years he had been here. "There has been the usual process of change," he said. "We have a lot of young people. Come and see tonight!"

He said that after the war, there were few baptisms compared to now. I asked how many there were now. "We keep no statistics." Yet he did have one statistic — the neighbouring church, one hundred and fifty yards away, has twenty times more baptisms than this parish. Why? "Each church has its own peculiarities. The neighbouring church is right next to a tram stop, so it is easier for people. But we will soon get more, because the city is building a new Metro station right next to us."

Accepting his invitation to return to worship, for three hours this evening we stood near the choir, separated from it only by a wooden barrier that was, in effect, an extension of the iconostasis. Through a slight opening I glimpsed a few of the singers — two women, several men, a boy in his late teens. There was a smaller choir on the opposite side of the church. Among the choristers was a girl of about ten with a face fresh as Eve's in the first week of creation.

The high point of the service was a funeral procession

100

through the church, the priests and deacons carrying an embroidered icon of the dead body of Jesus. Before the service started everyone had reverenced the life-size image. It had been placed in the centre of the church with masses of flowers all around. Four people carried the funeral pallet. The pastor walked underneath carrying the Gospels. Quite a lot of people, including many children, joined the procession.

I was surprised at how my own feelings were affected by this simple, austere ceremony. We were all caught up in the crucifixion and burial of Jesus. I found tears spilling out of my eyes, and was not alone in my grief.

The choir sang mournful, simple music. Though some of those in the choir are professional opera singers (the choir is well-known for its recordings), there is nothing operatic in the music of Good Friday.

There were several bursts of sung Alleluias during the service. Once again it impresses me that the Russian Orthodox Church, while quite capable of explaining what it does, prefers to *do* rather than to explain — to paint an icon rather than to publish a book about the Holy Trinity, to sing Alleluias at Jesus' funeral rather than to give a sermon about life after death.

Back in the hotel, reading a biography of St. Seraphim of Sarov, I found a stanza from a Russian song for Good Friday:

On a sunlit hill in Jerusalem
they hoisted up my Love.
In a Russian wood in the dead of night
I finished off the job.
Woe's me![2]

---

2. Julia de Beausobre, *Flame in the Snow* (Glasgow: Collins Sons & Co., 1979), with a new introduction by John Lawrence.

Moscow, April 18 Holy Saturday:

Volodya and I went to a morning church service in north-
east Moscow at the Church of St. John the Warrior. As we
arrived a deacon was singing in a deep bass voice from the
Book of Isaiah.

> Listen to me, O coastlands,
> and hearken, you peoples from afar.
> The Lord called me from the womb,
> from the body of my mother he named my name . . .
> And he said to me, You are my servant . . .
> I have graven you in the palms of my hands . . .
>
> Hearken to me, you who know righteousness,
> the people in whose heart is my law;
> fear not the reproach of men . . .
> For the moth shall eat them up like a garment,
> and the worm will eat them like wool;
> but my deliverance will be for ever,
> and my salvation to all generations . . .
>
> How beautiful upon the mountain
> are the feet of him who brings good tidings,
> who publishes peace, who brings good tidings of good,
> who publishes salvation,
> who says to Zion, Your God reigns . . .
>
> Who has believed what we have heard?
> And to whom has the arm of the Lord been revealed?
> For he grew up before him like a young plant,
> and like a root out of dry ground.
> He had no form or comeliness that we should look at him,
> and no beauty that we should desire him.
> He was despised and rejected by men;
> a man of sorrows, and acquainted with grief,
> and as one from whom men hide their faces
> and was despised, and we esteemed him not . . .

The chanting of Isaiah went on and on in the deacon's shifts.

We listened for an hour, then went back into central Moscow for a walk on Arbat Street, the only street in Moscow closed to traffic. The Arbat is old, relatively unspoiled, and lined with small stores that include quite a number of used-book shops. Volodya regularly searches for Pasternak's famous Russian translation of Shakespeare's plays. It was surprising to discover a number of religious books and old Bibles for sale. Despite the changes in progress in the USSR, religious books are not yet offered where new books are sold. The old Bibles were sold while we were there. Walking back toward Kalanin Prospekt, we had a cup of coffee made from beans ground while we watched — delicious!

Then we were off to the airport to catch our flight to Kiev.

Kiev, April 18:

"We have the proverb," Volodya told me, "that says 'your tongue will lead you to Kiev'. It is something like the saying in the west that all roads lead to Rome. Kiev is the mother of all Russian cities, the first fountain of our culture and language, and the place where Russia was baptized."

Most of the way the sky was clear. We had a fine view of rolling hills, huge forests, and snow-covered villages. I glimpsed horse-drawn sleds on forest tracks. As we got further south, the snow on the ground turned to patches. Finally, under a grey cliff of clouds, we could see Kiev, capital of the Ukraine and now the third largest city in the USSR, shining on steep hills over the Dnieper River.

We were met by Boris Udovenko, the priest I travelled with in February and whose home is Kiev. He hopes to be with us at least while we are in Kiev, and perhaps will be "blessed" by the Metropolitan to come with us to Odessa. We had both lost a few kilos since we were last together — "the mercy of Lent," he said.

We drove to a hotel, also named the Ukraina but this time *in* the Ukraine, had a light meal, and then Volodya and I were put under orders to nap in preparation for the all-night Easter service.

Kiev, Easter, April 19:

Christos Voskresey! Veyeastino voskresey! Christ is risen! Truly he is risen! I have heard and exchanged these words countless times in the past twelve hours, so often that the words seem to say themselves.

Just after ten, Boris, Volodya and I drove out to Boris' parish, Our Lady of the Protecting Veil, a brick church built in 1906 that stands on a hilltop on the west edge of Kiev. Though it was still half an hour before the service was due to start, there was a steady stream of people walking up the dark hillside. A policeman stood at the foot of the hill blocking the way to cars. An exception was made for us but only when the driver promised to bring the car back down after dropping us off.

Though it isn't a large church, there were at least two-thousand people jammed inside and as many around the church. Boris thought it best to put me on the altar side of the iconostasis where there was space and also a few chairs. I was, at first, disappointed. A true Russian Easter is spent standing in the crowd, not on the altar side of the iconostasis. But after the first hour I realized I wouldn't have lasted through the service otherwise. Apart from having to spend five hours on my feet when I would normally be sleeping, I would have suffered from claustrophobia. In fact at one point someone in the congregation reached her breaking point and started to scream. Space was made and friends got her outside where she could sit down and recover.

I was near the centre of the iconostasis, next to the Royal Doors, where I had a view of tables heaped with Easter bread — *kulich* — in the foreground and a sea of faces illumined by candle light.

The people who stood out the most from my vantage point

105

were a group of lanky teenagers who had apparently never been in church before — "window-shoppers," Volodya whispered to me. They didn't cross themselves, didn't bow, but behaved like passive spectators at a play. The women didn't wear scarfs. The tallest, a young woman, looked like her Dutch counterparts — short blonde hair cut in punkish style standing up from her head, and blue-shadowed eyes. The most striking thing about her was her alert eyes, round as saucers, watching everything with awe. Now and then she pointed out to her boyfriend something that had caught her attention. There was real excitement in her face, a deep engagement. Perhaps one day I will return here and find her wearing a scarf and crossing herself.

Volodya and I were not the only lay people behind the iconostasis. There were half a dozen old men who seemed to be fixtures of the parish. One had a white moustache spread across his face like the wings of a sea gull. Another walked slowly with a cane but stood throughout the service singing, in a rich bass voice, with the priests.

There were four priests, one deacon, and an acolyte. The dean, Fr. Nicholas, has a moustache and goatee. The oldest priest seemed paralyzed on one side yet managed both to stand and walk. More than anyone else, he directed the singing at the altar, starting off the special Easter hymns, indicating the rhythm with one hand, radiating delight. He offered many gestures of encouragement and appreciation.

At times it seemed like anarchy at the altar. Little whispers and much sign language about what to do next. One of the priests would start singing something loud and clear, another priest would cut him off with an urgent whisper, "Not yet, not yet!" Then someone else would take the lead. It was rather wild and disordered but amiable. No one seemed to mind.

Actually it wasn't Easter when the service began. Lent had another hour to run. Easter began with a sung announcement of the resurrection. The dean went out the royal doors into the congregation and sang out, "*Christos voskresey!*" Everyone responded in one voice, "*Veyeastino voskresey!*" It is impossible to put on paper how this sounds in the dead of night in a church overheated by crowds of people and hundreds of candles. It is like a shudder in the earth, the cracking open of the tomb. Then there was an explosion of bell-ringing. Russian bells sing their own Easter hymn in a particular pattern of sound that rejoices in the victory of life over death.

The congregation, singing an Easter hymn, followed the priests out of the church and circled the building in a slow procession. Those already outside, holding candles in their hands, parted to make way for the procession. The singing was continuous. All the while the bells were sounding out for miles around, in the deepest night, the news of the resurrection.

Finally the procession came back into the church. Once again there was hardly room to breathe. The priests arranged themselves in front of the iconostasis and sang the opening five verses of the Gospel According to St. John:

> In the beginning was the Word, and the Word was with God, and the Word was God. He was in the beginning with God. All things were made through him and without him was not anything made that was made. In him was life and the life was the light of men. The light shines in the darkness and the darkness has not overcome it.

This was done first in Church Slavonic, then in seven other languages: Ukrainian, Russian, Greek, Latin, English, French and German. More languages would have been used if they were known to any of the priests. ''The more languages we use in singing the Easter Gospel,'' Volodya said to me, ''the better we like it. I was in a Moscow church where they sang the Gospel in twelve languages. It makes the whole world present.''

As I stood in the sanctuary my eyes often rested on the icon of Mary with the Protecting Veil on the wall above the altar. Yes, I thought, she is not only the mother of Jesus but the mother of all believers. If we want, we can let her drape us in her protecting veil, the veil of God's love, the only real security we have, the only indestructible wall.

After the five-hour service — vespers, Easter proclamation,

morning prayer, Eucharist — the crowd outside parted to form a pathway about two yards wide which was lined with baskets full of food, each basket dominated by the Easter bread and lit by a candle struggling against the wind. There was still no hint of dawn in the sky. A priest lavishly dowsed every basket with water blessed at the Easter service, at the same time showering everything and everyone. So many people were there to have their Easter baskets blessed that the circles kept reforming. It took more than an hour for the four priests, working in turns, to bless every basket.

Even then the night was far from over. Next came a big meal. While the congregation walked back to the tables in their own homes, the priests and staff of the parish went into an old one-storey wooden building that clung precariously to the edge of the hill, the parish house, where meat and home-made sausage and Easter eggs and Easter bread awaited us.

We remained at the table until about 8 o'clock in the morning. It wasn't only food but drink — vodka, wine, Russian soft drinks and Pepsi Cola (the brand name in cyrillic letters and the contents bottled under US licence in the USSR). There were many toasts, including some to me and some to world peace, which I momentarily represented.

At some point I looked at all these men and women crowded around the table, laughing and telling stories, and found myself overcome by love for them, and stunned at the thought that they would be likely casualties in another world war. One of the people at the table was the choir director, who wore a well-tailored grey suit and had the look of an old English gentleman. Perhaps because he found out I sing in a choir and that two of my sons do also, there was a particular sense of connection between us. Before we parted this older man wept on my shoulder. I cried as well.

I wrote a message in the parish guest book. It has been little written in since it was started in 1974. The last entry before mine was from a group of British pilgrims that came to Kiev in 1984. Then I was given several loaves of Easter bread, a sack of beautifully coloured Easter eggs and an armful of flowers. As we left, I noticed people were already arriving for the morning service. The dawn had broken.

Utterly exhausted, Volodya and I went back to the hotel to sleep, but before going to my room I gave the woman at the desk on our floor some of the Easter eggs and one of the loaves of Easter bread. Overcoming worry that a religious greeting might offend her, I said, "*Christos Voskresey!*" She smiled and replied, "*Veyeastino voskresey!*

Kiev, 19 April, (afternoon):

After a nap and a meal, we went to Kiev's oldest surviving church, the Hagia Sophia (Holy Wisdom) Cathedral. It is a building inspired by what was once the church of Hagia Sophia (still existing but now a mosque) in Constantinople (now Istanbul).

Kiev's Hagia Sophia, dedicated in 1037, stands in a walled compound of ancient buildings. Though now a museum, the cathedral remains a remarkable building, and a lucky one at that despite the liturgical vacuum inside. Surviving all the wars and catastrophies of the last nine hundred and fifty years, it is not only intact but unspoiled.

"Our city has had many uninvited visitors," said Boris. "In the thirteenth century, the Tartars conquered Kiev and enslaved the survivors. There were only two hundred houses left standing. Nearly all the churches were destroyed, including the Church of the Holy Virgin, the first stone church built after Kiev's conversion. In later centuries the Poles, Lithuanians and Germans have been here. The Tartars and Germans were the most merciless. Our city has been under the rule of others for at least two hundred years of its history. We had many defeats, but some victories too. In 1709, in this church, Peter the Great celebrated his triumph in the Battle of Poltava over Charles XII and the Swedish army."

Mosaics and frescoes dating from the time the church was built are still to be seen, including a large mosaic of Mary that dominates the nave. It is the image of Mary called the Indestructible Wall. She is wearing royal purple robes and stands against a background of luminous gold with her hands raised in a priestly gesture of prayer and blessing.

Once one of Europe's largest buildings, the cathedral is a house of many mansions. We spent more than an hour

110

'The purpose of our art is to lead us from what can be seen to what cannot be seen.' An icon painter at the Holy Trinity-Saint Sergius Lavra outside Moscow. *October 15, 1984.*

Icons such as Our Lady of Vladimir are distinguished from others by a Russian word meaning 'tender loving.' This icon is venerated as the greatest holy treasure of the nation. *October 21, 1984.*

Rublev's Holy Trinity icon. 'The three are so engaged with each other that there is an overwhelming oneness . . . and you are invited to be present in their love, to be forgiven and healed and saved in their love.' *October 21, 1984.*

'Icons aren't decorations, but a reflection that God became man. They are holy doors.' Father Zinon, icon painter and monk of the Pskovo-Pechorsky Monastery. *February 25, 1987.*

Poster for the film *Repentance*. 'What good is a street that doesn't take you to a church?' *April 22, 1987.*

'Before coming to the seminary, I was a nuclear physicist. Had things gone a little differently, I would probably be making nuclear weapons now.' Father Nicholas Preobrajensk, assistant rector of the Leningrad Theological Seminary. *February 21, 1987.*

'To learn about the church, I borrowed atheist books and found parts that helped me, though the books themselves weren't very deep. Atheism can't really influence anyone. It can't answer the deepest questions. It can't give a direction in life.' Father Germann, monk. *March 1, 1987.*

Two young people, one of them a soldier, on Easter Sunday near the Monastery of the Caves, Kiev. *April 10, 1987.*

'As long as we have been living here, there has been constant prayer.' Erguminay Margarita, Mother Superior of Pokorvskye Convent, Kiev. *April 20, 1987.*

'There is never a bad meal when there is vodka on the table.'
Easter meal with Lydia, Sevya and Father Boris Udovenko at
their home in the Podol district of Kiev. *April 22, 1987*.

'Christ didn't say thinking is the way. He said love is the way.' Father Alexi, monk at the Holy Trinity Lavra, Zagorsk, standing in the rain.
July 21, 1987.

'I fell asleep in my illness and had a dream in which I was walking on railroad tracks that extended infinitely into the dark.' Ludmilla Tyschuk preparing lunch in a Moscow apartment.
July 23, 1987.

'I was baptized in boiling water.' Father Victor Bekarevitch being embraced by Bishop Constantine at the Alexander Nevsky Church, Minsk. *July 28, 1987.*

Under crowns suggesting the dignity of marriage, a young couple are wed in the Russian Orthodox Church.
Credit: Publishing Department, Moscow Patriarchate.

About 200 people a week — well over 10,000 a year — are baptized at the Holy Trinity Cathedral in Leningrad. *Credit: World Council of Churches.*

Russian Orthodox members are asked to receive the Eucharist 'at least four times a year and to prepare beforehand for at least two days. It has to be something special.' *Credit: Publishing Department, Moscow Patriarchate.*

A crowded Cathedral of the Assumption, Smolensk, at Sunday liturgy. 'No one hushed the children.' *July 26, 1987.*

exploring it, finding level upon level, hidden stairways, balconies, new rooms and halls suddenly appearing. The cathedral gives the impression of being infinite in size, a model of heaven. Its thirteen cupolas represent Jesus and the apostles.

We paused at the tomb of Vladimir's son, Yaroslav the Wise, who presided over the building of Hagia Sophia. He was supreme sovereign of Russian lands until his death in 1054. "It is said that Yaroslav often read until late into the night," Volodya mentioned. "He founded a school for five-hundred students."

We went on to St. Andrew's, a small Baroque church rising to a dramatic height on the brow of a steep hill. One of the many casualties of the Khrushchev period, it was closed is 1962, as was the associated seminary. The painting of the iconostasis is more Italian than Russian. St. Andrew's is, architecturally, just barely a Russian church. Now one of the treasures of Kiev, it must have been a rude shock to traditionalists when it first opened for worship in 1761.

We proceeded to the monument to Prince Vladimir on the edge of the hill where Kiev took root. Vladimir is shown holding aloft a cross.

"It was Vladimir's grandmother, Olga, who wanted Russia to be Christian," Boris said, "but it was Vladimir that made Russia Christian. Without Olga perhaps it wouldn't have happened. In the Russian Church we call her Equal of the Apostles. The ancient chronicles speak of her as 'the dawn in the morning that announces the sun.' On her feast day we sing, 'Having covered herself with the wings of prudence, she flew above the visible creatures; having sought God and the Creator and having found him, she was reborn by baptism. Having tasted of the tree of life, she is forever incorruptible.' "

In the Primary Chronicle of early Russian history, the *Tale of Bygone Times* compiled by the Kievan monk, St. Nestor, Vladimir is presented as a ruler who knew that the time had come to embrace a great religious tradition. Taking great care to make the right choice, he sent emissaries to investigate the religions of neighbouring countries. They went to synagogues, mosques, and to both Latin and Byzantine Christian churches.

111

Receiving Vladimir's representatives in Constantinople, the Patriarch ordered the clergy assembled in Hagia Sophia for a festive service. Incense filled the air. Choirs sang. According to Nestor's Chronicle, the emissaries wrote to Vladimir:

> We knew not whether we were in heaven or on earth, for on earth there is no such splendour or such beauty, and we are at a loss how to describe it. We only know that God dwells among these people and that their services are fairer than the ceremonies of other nations. We can never forget that beauty.

As much as in the water of the Dnieper, in those clouds of incense in Constantinople, Russia became Orthodox.

With Vladimir's statue behind us, we went down the steep embankment past young couples enjoying the spring weather Easter had brought to the city. The path ended at a spot, marked by a second monument, where a small stream flows into the Dnieper. On a June day in 988, the people of Kiev, carrying banners and icons, went in procession from the Church of the Prophet Elijah to this very place and were baptized. "Joy was seen throughout heaven at the sight of so many souls being saved," Nestor records in the Chronicle. That same summer Christian conversion spread to the cities of Novgorod, Rostov, Vladimir and Belgorod.

"Before his conversion Vladimir was far from a saintly man," Boris said. "The Chronicle says he was 'a man insatiable in vice.' But after his conversion he became renowned for his care of the poor, of orphans and the sick. The palace gates were opened to the hungry. He built hospices for the aged. He opposed torture and execution of criminals. We regard him as a saint, not only for opening the door of faith for us but for the life he led as a believer. The cathedral of Kiev is named after him.

Boris is named after one of Vladimir's sons. "Prince Boris and his younger brother, Prince Gleb," said Boris, "were both murdered by an ambitious elder brother, Sviatopolk. Neither resisted their brother. They were the first to be canonized in the Russian church. We call them 'Passion Bearers'."

The Dnieper, Europe's third longest river, rises in a peat bog in the hills north-west of Smolensk and, fourteen hundred miles to the south, empties into the Black Sea. The river was a major link in a system of waterways providing a route "from the Varangians to the Greeks." Artifacts unearthed by archaeologists working along the Dnieper come from the Swedish as well as Byzantine sources. Kiev, at the river's middle point, stands at the heart of the main highway of Russian development.

"According to legend," Boris said, "in the first century the river was the route followed by one of the Apostles, St. Andrew, who paused where we are standing and prophesied, 'Do you see these hills? The grace of God will shine on them. A great city will be built with many churches praising God within its walls.' Then he planted a cross on the hilltop above us where the Monastery of the Caves was founded nine centuries later. In the statue, the cross Andrew left is in Vladimir's arms."

Following the stream to the banks of the Dnieper, we went on to a place nearby where a monument has been erected commemorating the sister and three brothers who founded Kiev. The sister — young, daring, unarmed — stands on the prow of a Viking-like long boat, her cloak flying in the wind, her arms out as if she is about to leap into the air. Her three brothers stand in the back of the boat, armed, fierce, searching the shoreline. It is from Ki, oldest of the brothers, that Kiev takes its name.

Climbing up the steep hill beneath the monastery, we stopped on the way by a large bed of red tulips where a soldier and his girl friend let me take their photo. She gave me her address, asking that I send her a print. Further on we came upon several boys on skate boards skilfully weaving through an obstacle course of empty Pepsi bottles, the sort of scene I associate more with California than the Ukraine. At last, out of breath and tired, we reached the walls of the Monastery of the Caves, its golden cupolas gleaming in the late afternoon sunlight. We will visit it tomorrow.

113

Kiev, Easter Monday, April 20:

On our way to the Convent of the Protecting Veil of the Mother of God (Pokrovskye), we talked about the convent's name, a title of Mary used by many Russian Orthodox churches. "We received it from the Greeks and it has become one of the main feast days in our Church," Boris said, "but over the centuries it disappeared from Greek church life, perhaps because of living under Moslem domination. It survives only in Russia, especially here in the Ukraine."

The convent's main church is huge and wide open, unencumbered by walls and pillars. It is beautifully painted from floor to ceiling with frescoes of saints and biblical scenes. Olga and Vladimir were painted on the wall up by the high balcony where the main part of the nuns' choir was singing.

Liturgically, the second day of Easter is hardly different from the first, except everyone has had a good night's sleep and so continues the celebration more rested. Boris was one of the celebrating priests, assisting Kiev's Metropolitan, Fileret, who had come to share Easter with the nuns. Volodya and I were led to a choir stall. It is raised, so I had a good view of the congregation. As usual, women were in the majority, but there were older men and quite a sprinkling of children who had come with their mothers or grandparents. Young adults were the rarities. Easter Monday isn't a holiday. Students had returned to their classrooms and working-age people were back at their jobs.

One of the old men wore a monk's fur cap. The Monastery of the Caves, Kiev's only religious community for men, was closed in Khrushchev's time, but reportedly some of the monks remain in Kiev and continue living the monastic life. I assume this was one of them. He had a face of the most astonishing innocence with very open, undefended eyes. He gazed freely at whatever interested him — for a time, at me. I thought at first he might be annoyed by my camera and my obvious interest in him but his face was absolutely calm with a gentleness of countenance I have never seen before, not in Russia, not anywhere.

About seventy of the convent's ninety-five members were in the church. Others were out in the carillon ringing bells that made me want to dance. (Later I noticed a professional sound engineer with a directional microphone down by the carillon taping the music; the Soviet record company, Melodya, has produced a number of recordings of church bells as well as church choral music.) Other nuns were in the kitchens preparing the meal.

There was a procession around the church differing from the procession of Easter night only in that this was in bright sunlight. The nuns carried banners of Mary and Jesus, and a large Easter bread, a candle in a glass chamber, and a cross. The bells were ringing continuously and holy water was flying every direction. Over and over we were singing the exclamations of Easter: "Christ is risen! Truly he is risen!"

I last watched Metropolitan Fileret celebrate the Liturgy at the Danilov Monastery in Moscow during the Peace Forum in February. His manner refreshed me then and did so again today. Every gesture is done with such attention and gentleness. It is part of the ritual to kiss each garment before it is put on. He does this with the devotion or a mother kissing a child on forehead at bed time. Every motion underlines the fact that we are in sacred space and sacred time.

One of the deacons assisting the Metropolitan, a big man with a dark brown beard, has a voice that can hardly be less immense and rich than was Caruso's. When he steps out from the Sanctuary and sings "Wisdom! Be Attentive!", it is the voice of the Archangel Gabriel, able to raise the dead. There was one nun with a voice to match but of nightingale quality.

In the afternoon, after lunch at the convent with the Metropolitan, we went to the Percherskaya Lavra, the Monastery of the Caves, the first monastic community in Russia though at present a museum.

Unfortunately, the main church, the eleventh century Cathedral of the Assumption, was dynamited by Germans soldiers shortly after the 791-day Occupation of Kiev began in 1941. All but one corner of the church was reduced to rubble.

We spent a long time in one church that survived the Occupation. A Russian tourist group was in it when we arrived, admiring four large frescoes by Ishkevich and Popov that show the Nativity, Jesus multiplying the loaves, Jesus preaching the Sermon on the Mount, and the Resurrection. The guide was talking, and there was a lot of moving about, every sound magnified and sifted together in the rich acoustic of the church. But when the group left there was a profound, sweet silence. Boris whispered: "Quietness! Can you hear the quietness? It's unbelievable!"

We went down the hillside until we came to a small church where a stairway descends into the earth. Thus we entered into the monastery's famous caves where thousands are buried, mainly monks, more than a hundred of whom have been canonized. The bodies of the saints, in glass-topped coffins, have mummified. The visitor sees the parchment-like hands, while the rest of the body is under silk cloth. The air is cool but not cold, and very fresh and sweet.

For tourists, the caves, with all their bones and mummies, provide a fascinating look at death. For believers the caves are an underground city of saints. One of those buried in the caves is the chronicler and biographer, St. Nestor, who died in 1113. A guide book notes, "The whole Orthodox world bows before the relics of the saints of the monastery; in times past and today, their blessing emanates undiminished upon all who come to their tombs in faith and love."[3]

In former times monks were guides, and visitors found their way with candles. The monks are gone and now the caves are lit by electric lights, but prayer continues in the caves. Many pause and cross themselves at each saint's body. We stopped and prayed with one couple, members of Boris'

3. Victor and Jennifer Louis, *The complete Guide Book to the Soviet Union* (London: Michael Joseph Publishers, 1980), p. 147.

parish, who were quietly singing Easter hymns before the body of St. Anthony, who, with St. Theodosius, founded the monastery in 1051.

"Public prayer didn't used to be allowed," said Boris, "but now they don't stop it. We would say to them, why not? If it is just words, what difference is it whether it is the words of a tourist guide or words of prayer from a believer? What difference if it is only words? So what does it matter?"

The monastery is on two adjacent hill tops, the higher hill supporting the larger and older part of the monastery. This was made into a museum many years ago, with the monks confined to the lower hill. But in 1962 the monks were ordered to leave altogether and the buildings on the lower hill left to rot. The church is completely decayed inside, but restoration has begun. A new roof is finished and has gleaming golden cupolas. Perhaps the millennium of the church will be the occasion for the Kiev authorities to allow monastic life to resume at least on this hilltop.

We went to St. Vladimir's Cathedral for the evening service, always a special one on Easter Monday, with most of the priests of the city coming to greet the Metropolitan. There were thirty priests and at least five thousand people. It is a large church, built in the late nineteenth century but in the Byzantine tradition and decorated in the most captivating way. Foremost is the famous painting of Mary, by Victor Vasnetsov. Both Mary and her child seem to be looking directly at each person in the church. Jesus' arms are open. It is quite an experience to stand in front of this — one sees why this is among of the most frequently seen icons in Russian homes.

The high point of the service was the reflection on Easter by Metropolitan Fileret delivered as he stood at the centre of the iconostasis. Speaking without notes, he started off by pushing away the praise which had just been heaped on him in a speech from his coadjutor bishop.

"The Holy Fathers said you have to ignore praise — it can lead you the wrong way," said the Metropolitan. "I have to hear only the good wishes underneath what my brother said.

117

Good wishes are nice and we all are glad to have them, but it's very important never to believe you are more important or higher than anyone else. I have to say this to my brother bishop and to all of you.

"It is Easter and I am thinking about what has inspired believers in our church during the last one thousand years. Today is exactly the day when we must ask the question, like believers before us: Why are we living on the earth? Why are we working hard? Why are we trying to have a good time? Why are we suffering? What is the meaning of life?

"There are many theories, many explanations from all the philosophers, but none of them fulfil us. All of them stop at the point of death. But our soul longs to keep living. It wants to be eternal. It wants to live without end. Life has meaning only if there is eternal life. If there isn't eternal life, no matter how beautiful your life, at the end it is just poor life.

"It's a pity sometimes to stand before a dead person who worked hard in life, did good works, suffered, was in many battles, but in the end saw no meaning, and he is dead and no one can help him. Great Solomon wisely said that the living dog is more blessed than the dead human.

"So we are happy, we are blessed, because we believe in eternal life. We know that the life of people is not life only until death. The soul doesn't disappear. It lives. It lives forever. This is so whether you believe it or not and it is true whether you want it or not, true whether you are a believer or an unbeliever. So no matter what kind of life you lived before death, you enter eternal life, and not only your soul but your body. We come into eternal life in both body and soul.

"Today we celebrate the Resurrection of Jesus Christ and we rejoice in it. And we see in it not only his resurrection but *our* resurrection. The Resurrection of Jesus Christ is the same as our resurrection. We believe that. We believe that in Christ each one of us will stand up.

"Many people do not believe in the Resurrection of Jesus Christ or in the Resurrection of anyone. I don't want to give them proof or argue with them. The main thing about their conviction, the thing their unbelief is founded on, is that it's impossible for a dead person to come back to life. How can it happen? How can something that is just dust and bones live again? And what about bodies that are now only ashes? Or were cut into many pieces? Or were eaten by beasts or fish? How can such people's bodies be made whole and come back to life? Our brain can't overcome this dilemma. How is it possible?

"But then we can ask another question: What about everything that exists? All this beauty? There are so many things we don't understand and can't explain. Most things we can't explain. What do you think? Isn't this huge miracle we live in as big a miracle as the Resurrection? Do you think creation is easier than resurrection? If God is strong enough to create everything from nothing, to create the whole world and the whole universe, do you think it is difficult to resurrect what he has already created?

"So don't be discouraged by anyone who says it's impossible. God has the strength to create everything.

"So, brothers and sisters, we believe in eternal life. But it isn't an easy belief. It is a belief that gives us responsibilities. We have to realize that each person, whether or not he wants God, must answer to God for his life — what he did, what he didn't do. He must stand judgement.

"It is a weakness not to believe in eternal life. Even if you don't believe, it is no justification when you stand before God with sins and horrible deeds. Don't imagine that you will be unjudgeable.

"Our people have lived by great ideals. The big ideal that has been living in our people for a thousand years is to live in God's truth. Not human truth. God's truth. Our ancestors mostly wanted to live according to God's truth. They suffered greatly. Many terrible things happened. There were dreadful persons. But somehow, no matter what sorrows there were, they were still trying to live according to God's truth.

"We need this too. God's truth has to lead us. We have to have a spiritual life even if we are surrounded by an unspiritual life. We need to have Christian families even if

119

we are surrounded by families that are breaking down. We need to work hard and sincerely, not for praise or money, but for the heart and soul of our neighbours. We have to work for our people.

"Let us not think about bread for ourselves. Bread is something we need, yes, but the person who thinks about bread for himself has lost the spiritual dimension of life. But if he thinks of bread for his neighbours, then he is leading a spiritual life — a life of love, a life of caring for others. This is the spiritual life.

"The Resurrection of Jesus Christ is not only a joy for us, it is a great responsibility and a great labour. It leads us to prepare for the Last Judgement. Let the Resurrection fill our hearts with belief in eternal life so that truth can take root in our hearts. Let us not only think about it in our minds but feel it in our hearts."

He was silent and then the people responded in one voice, "*Spasi gospodi*!" — God save you! The Russian word for thank-you — *spasiba* — has the same root. Then came a time to greet the Metropolitan. Everyone in the congregation waited their turn. This was still going on when we left an hour later.

Kiev, 21 April:

Last night I noticed two girls who brought flowers to Metropolitan Fileret. I discovered today they have Boris as their godfather. Boris says, "Nicholas, their father, has sat at my table many times. He used to throw a lot of snow at my wisdom! He and his wife, Tayisa, wanted children but a long time passed and there were none. Then she had a daughter, Maryechka, who is ten now, and a year later there was Olga."

We spent much of the day at the Florovsky Monastery, a baroque place, quite simple, rather poor. It is a community of eighty nuns, some very young, some ancient. On a wall near the church's entrance, there is a life-sized icon of St. Seraphim of Sarov on the rock in the forest where he prayed for a thousand days. Many people kiss the icon before entering the church.

Again we were with Metropolitan Fileret. A large crowd was waiting outside the church, bells ringing for him as soon as his car came through the monastery gate. A nun stood inside the church door to offer him the traditional symbols of welcome, bread and salt. The sisters sang a special song

Hanging from the ceiling of the church was a large candelabra filled with burning candles. There is a large painting on the church wall of Mary, Joy of the Sorrowful. She is crowned and has a crowned baby Jesus on her lap, while around them all sorts of people are on their knees. White streamers represent their prayers.

In the Orthodox Liturgy, the entire congregation sings the Beatitudes, the Credo, and the Our Father. This is done with a drum-beat, heart-beat rhythm. No matter how big, the church always seems too small to contain the sound. These are among the moments in the Liturgy when a visitor experiences tangibly, physically, the strength of belief. Apart from the kettle-drum impact of each syllable, the chant is similar to Gregorian chant used in monasteries of the Catholic Church in the west. I sang along quietly with the bits of Slavonic I have learned or can roughly imitate.

I noticed the faithful bow their heads at certain points in the liturgy, for example when the gospel is read; also when the priest says, "*Mir vsyem!*" This means, "Peace be with you!" There is an exchange between the priest and the congregation when he comes out from the sanctuary shortly before the canon prayer and says, "Forgive me, my children!" The people respond, "God will forgive!"

Though the congregation was mainly old women, there were younger people in the back of the church who had arrived just as the service was about to start. Children were mainly with their grandparents, though later in the service, younger mothers made their way to the front so that their children could receive communion. While adults rarely receive communion in most Orthodox churches, the infants and children receive often. I thought of the verse, "Let the children come unto me, and hinder them not . . . "

The children always catch a lot of my attention. They are usually quite focused on the Liturgy, watching everything and crossing themselves. If they are in the same family, they often hold hands or rest against each other. Today there were two sisters at the front, both in old clothing — I am tempted to say poor, but in fact well-kept hand-me-down clothing.

The nuns wear a beehive-shaped head covering. Their faces and hands are all that isn't covered. Some of them prayed the rosary during the liturgy. I noticed a variety of rosaries, not only the black silk ones I'm familiar with but other colours, and in one case a rosary of silver beads with a magenta tassel — this in the hands of one of the elderly sisters.

Tolya, a photographer, whom Volodya and I met yesterday and stayed up with last night, was also at the monastery. He is tall, with a face several days removed from a razor. He spent the Liturgy photographing shy nuns, something few photographers would dare and which the nuns normally wouldn't allow, but Tolya has the Metropolitan's blessing and takes pictures with a quiet authority that matches a Russian crossing himself. He got right up in the choir box on the right side of the church, set up his tripod though there wasn't much space for him, still less for his tripod, and spent two hours photographing the nuns singing.

One jarring event in the Liturgy was the Metropolitan turning away one of those who had lined up to receive communion. Perhaps because she had such an angry expression, the Metropolitan asked her something — Boris guessed it was to find out if she had been to confession. She responded with an abrupt gesture that said No. Then she walked away, furious.

Walking out of the church through the sacristy, one of the nuns asked to see my Nikon camera. It was clear she had never before had a close look at such a machine. She held it every which way. To show how it was used, I took a photo of another nun standing in the adjacent doorway.

We were invited to eat lunch at the convent. Metropolitan Fileret was at the head of the table and at his side another bishop, Basil, who was born in the Ukraine but left with his family just after the Revolution. For many years the United States has been his home — he is in the Soviet Union only for the third time since he was a child, and these few visits only in the last few years. He is tall and has a flowing white beard. His face is austere but welcoming.

Apart from his own snow white beard, Metropolitan Fileret has a child's face, hardly lined, with clear, expectant eyes that have a quiet curiosity in them, alert but not prying. He has a remarkable stillness. Nothing about him indicates hurry. He doesn't play the part of the consequential executive with urgent matters to tend to at his desk.

The table conversation was on many topics — the nuclear disaster at Chernobyl, the AIDS epidemic now beginning to find victims in the USSR, factory-raised chickens who spend their lives imprisoned in tiny cages, the history of atheism, Baptist influence on Russia, Peter the Great, and western countries in which credit cards have inaugurated debt as a lifestyle.

"People may not believe in eternal life," said Metropolitan Fileret, "but they certainly believe in eternal debt!" People are in debt, but nations even more in debt, mainly because of the costs of the arms race. The Metropolitan remarked that while the US and the USSR had been preoccupied with military competition, Japan — freed from militarization by the treaty it signed at the end of the war — had been producing things people want and can use, and that the Japanese economy was flourishing.

"Food," he said, "is becoming another factory-product that looks better than it tastes, like American strawberries, which are a pale imitation of real garden strawberries. Now food, even though it looks good, can have things in it that are bad for you."

In the afternoon we first went to Babi Yar, a ravine west of Kiev where between a hundred thousand and two hundred thousand people, mainly Jews, were executed by the German army. In the sixties Yevtushenko wrote a poem that began with the comment that there was no monument at Babi Yar. Yevtushenko was revolted with the renaissance of anti-semitism and identified himself with its victims:

. . . I seem to be a Jew.
Here I plod through ancient Egypt.
Here I perish crucified on the cross,
and to this day I bear the scars of nails . . .

I seem to be Anne Frank
transparent as a branch in April . . .

The wild grasses rustle over Babi Yar.
The trees look ominous, like judges.
Here all things scream silently, and, baring my head,
slowly I feel myself turning grey.
And I myself am one massive, soundless scream
above the thousand thousand buried here.
I am each old man here shot dead.
I am every child here shot dead.[4]

4. Yevgeny Yevtushenko, "Babi Yar," *The Poetry of Yevgeny Yevtushenko*, ed. and trans. George Reavey (London: Marion Boyars Publishers, 1981), pp. 147 and 149.

In 1976, perhaps in answer to Yevtushenko's celebrated poem, a monument was erected commemorating all those murdered here. The figures are shown in the last moments of life. An old woman stood next to us crying, her face buried in her hands.

Then we went to the church of St. Cyril of Alexandria, a twelfth century building still possessing many of the original frescoes, but also graced with a remarkable iconostasis done by Mikhael Vrubel in 1884. In Vrubel's work, Jesus and Mary are unmistakably Jewish: semitic features, and skin many shades darker than Ukrainian. It must have enraged anti-Semites. How appropriate that it is near Babi Yar.

I had an hour in the Russian Museum. The painting that impressed me most was Ilya Repin's life-sized portrait of a nun — a woman of stunning intelligence, faith, and modesty. Reproductions in books hadn't prepared me for the actual painting.[5] Near it was Nikolai Yarshenko's painting of a woman student walking through the rain in Leningrad. She could be the nun, but some years earlier in life. What immense resolve in her face! One doesn't sense faith — or at least not religious faith — but perhaps a conviction that she will spend her life working for justice.[6]

There is a painting by Nikolai Ghe of Christ's face while he was being crucified — white face, red and blue bruises in the face — all in abrupt strokes as if the painting itself were done on the cross rather than an easel. Ghe's Christ suffers pain of body and spirit as deeply as anyone who has ever known agony.

There is a painting by Lerov of a Holy Fool, life-size and life-like. He is a grinning man, in bare feet and gray rags, with a large iron cross around his neck standing before a broken fence. It is winter. The sun is about to rise and there are birds in the air — as if to say, here is someone people call insane, a man living a bird's life outside the usual fences,

5. Reproduced in *Ilya Repin*, ed. by Gregori Sternin (Leningrad: Aurora Art Publishers, 1985), plate 102.

6. *The Itinerants,* compiled and introduced by Andrei Lebedev (Leningrad: Aurora Art Publishers, 1982), plate 111.

125

a life given meaning and warmth only because of the resurrection that is suggested by the sun that is just beginning to rise.

Another Repin painting is of St. Nicholas. No Santa Claus, he is in his bishop's vestments stopping the execution of three condemned people. He has put his hand on the blade of the executioner's sword while a man kneels prayerfully on the ground, waiting to die. The powerful, pirate-like executioner is stunned. In the background there is a Roman legionnaire and a standard representing the power of the state. Nicholas was, no doubt, a kind of holy fool too, getting in the way of things, calling on the executioner to disobey those who gave him his orders, and in the process risking his own life. It is an image of a Christ-like church that risks everything for the victims.[7]

Also by Repin is a study of the crucifixion. One of the thieves is naked and in agony on the cross, another is being bloodily nailed to the cross. Jesus, standing with dignity under a massive crown of thorns, is being stripped. There is a group of several women on the left pleading, like Nicholas, with a soldier but the soldier has thrown out his hands in such a way that you can hear him say, "What can I do? I'm only following orders."[8]

Volodya and I spent Tuesday evening at Boris' house in Podol, the lower part of Kiev. Going by tram, we walked up a dirt road to a particular gateway, passed through a small garden, patted the dog, and entered an old wooden house in which the floors seem to follow the curve of the hill. Lydia, his wife, was busy finishing a salad. Their ten-year-old son, Sevya, greeted us in a tee-shirt that said "Ban the Bomb" in English.

The porch has been windowed in to become a dining room. The late afternoon light illuminated a long table covered with Easter eggs, Easter bread, all sorts of sausages, sliced meat, sliced fish, stuffed eggs made to look like red-topped mushrooms, and salads. There were many bottles — mineral

7. Ibid., plates 112, 113.
8. Ibid., plate 159; also note other studies in this series, plates 109, 110, 111, 160.

water, Pepsi Cola, several varieties of vodka, cognac from Armenia, Russian champagne, and wine both home-made and from Ukrainian vineyards. Still there was room for flowers and other decorations.

Lydia has black hair and a round, open face. She and Boris gave us a tour of the ramshackle house that has no right angles. It's a pity the old houses in this neighbourhood are slated for destruction as the expanding modern city chews up village fragments that survive. Boris and Lydia have been here twelve years and hope for another two before the house succumbs to architectural euthanasia. Under two icons that face their bed, I noticed a beautiful Palekh box similar to the one in our bedroom in Holland. I felt more at home than they could imagine.

Music, provided most of the evening by a cassette tape recorder, ranged from Easter hymns sung by a Russian Orthodox choir to Johnny Cash and American black spirituals. Here in Kiev we were hearing Barbara Hendricks singing, "I'm so glad I got my religion in time!"

We were joined by a widowed priest, Alexander Kubelius, and another priest and his wife, Nicholas and Tayisa Zapparozhetz, and their two daughters, Maryechka and Olga, the same ones who gave flowers to Metropolitan Fileret on Monday. As at the cathedral, both had ribbons in their hair and wore identical dresses. They look like twins.

There mother, Tayisa, has fair hair pulled straight back and shy eyes. She grew up in the nearby Florovsky Convent where her father was priest. Her first thirty years were largely spent at the convent. "It was better growing up in a convent than anywhere I can imagine," she said as we were eating Easter eggs and sipping lemon vodka. "There were many children living there, or nearby, and we could go where we liked, and we could go into the church anytime and pray. I liked to get up at five in the morning so I could take part in the first prayer service, especially on days when I was preparing for Holy Communion." Having married a priest, she isn't so far from the convent life even now.

Fr. Nicholas is a huge man, with a thick, close-cropped

brown beard, many gold teeth, and a gift as a story teller.
Among the drinks on the table was a large pitcher of
homemade *kvas*. Noticing how much I like it, Fr. Nicholas
told a story about a wealthy man who was passing through
a Ukrainian village and stayed for the night in a peasant's
house. Amazed at how good the *kvas* was, he asked a child
at the table if there was enough for him to bring a few bottles
home. "Oh yes, sir, lots and lots. I know because the other
day, when a mouse fell into it, Mother got in the vat to fetch
it out and the *kvas* was right up to her waist."

Borscht was served, which inspired Nicholas to tell a story
about a man who came to a certain house to beg for food.
"Well," said the woman at the door, "how do you like day-
old soup?" "That would be fine." "Okay, then come back
tomorrow."

Nicholas told a story of his childhood. "I was watching my
mother colour Easter eggs. It was the final hours before Easter
after all those weeks of fasting. So many days without eating
one egg! At that moment nothing seemed so delicious as a
hard boiled egg. I asked her whether I could be allowed to
eat any eggs that happened to be cracked? Absolutely not.
Soon afterward the rest of the family went to church for the
Easter vigil, but I had no shoes and I was very little so I had
to stay at home. Before leaving, my mother warned me about
the eggs, 'If you eat even one egg before Easter, you will die.'
I struggled hard against temptation for about an hour, but
when I noticed an egg with a broken shell, I lost the struggle.
After swallowing the last bite, it hit me that I would soon die,
so I reasoned, 'Why not eat some more? It no longer makes
any difference.' I managed to eat ten, then I lay down, waiting
for death. In fact, the way my stomach felt, it was obvious
death was near. This is how my family found me when they
got home, me at death's door, and ten Easter eggs missing.
But I was lucky. Mother felt she couldn't punish me, it being
Easter. For three days I was a prisoner in the house. But I
lived!"

After hearing about a half dozen such stories, I said that
it seemed that to be a priest in the Russian Orthodox Church,

you had to be able to make people laugh. "At least to be married to a priest," Lydia responded, "you need a sense of humour!"

Boris poured some special vodka made with honey. We all tasted it carefully. "There is no such thing as bad vodka," said Boris. "There is never a bad meal when there is vodka on the table," Fr. Nicholas added. Then he told a vodka story: "At the cost of millions of dollars, the United Nations finally got a translating computer. The day came when at last it was installed. The press was there. Many television cameras. To demonstrate the brilliant computer, the Secretary General decided to show how it could translate from Russian to English. He chose the Russian words for 'The Spirit is willing but the flesh is weak.' This was no problem for the computer. Immediately it printed out in English: 'The vodka is agreeable but the meat isn't so good.' "

Mention of the United Nations inspired Fr. Nicholas to talk about destruction of the environment. "Only man is a threat to nature," he said. "All these things people do to damage the earth! Computers and atom bombs are from the devil! Once the lion and the lamb could dwell together in peace and now everything is being poisoned to death. Nature calls us to help her. We Christians must say, 'Come God to save us.' "

Thinking of how much I depend on a computer in my own work, I said that sometimes computers aren't so bad. "Maybe you're right," he said apologetically. "I still live in an age when the atom wasn't divided."

Fr. Alexander spoke about being in the army and how important it had been to meet people from different religions. At that time he was just beginning to be an Orthodox believer. "In fact, in those early days of belief, I was very rigid about my religious views and one night got into a big argument with another soldier about the Mother of God. But the other soldier finally said, 'I am your brother, a Baptist. Let's not quarrel.' And that was the end of it. We became close friends."

He talked about war toys and how important it is for parents not to bring them into the home. There was a baptism he did recently where a toy gun had been brought along by one of the children. He asked the parents to take it away before going on with the sacrament. "Symbols are so important. Not only Christians, no one should buy such symbols. In fact they shouldn't be made."

Fr. Nicholas told a story about how Peter the Great had liked statues of Roman deities. "But finally he got rid of them because a certain bishop wouldn't visit him so long as such statues were in the palace. Whenever I go to someone's apartment to do a baptism, if I see such an idol, even though the people living there consider it as a decoration, I ask them to get rid of it. I tell them this story and I say, 'I am not a bishop and you aren't Peter the Great, but we can follow their example.''

"Ukrainians are a singing people," Volodya had told me on the flight to Kiev. "They sing even more than Russians do." As it got dark, and when most of the eating was over, Fr. Nicholas began to sing and everyone joined in — even me, as best I could, as the tunes were catchy and I could pick up some of the refrains. It was wonderful, soulful music. Ukrainian ballads are gentle, romantic, poignant and long, and are sung from the heart.

After a lot of singing and more drinking, Fr. Nicholas got quite grave and said to me, "I want to say to our guest, if you think perhaps priests are too light-hearted in the Russian Orthodox Church, and I admit sometimes we are, remember that in Lent we don't even watch the news on television. For seven weeks no meat, no milk products. This is our tradition — it isn't something we are proud of but it is the way we live. We keep it strictly. We all pray, the children too. We don't make them. We just do it. We want to do it. And the children come to father or mother and ask them for a blessing. But now it's Easter, and this is Easter life!"

We went downstairs to a room where there was a piano. Tayisa and her daughters played, and Fr. Nicholas, despite the smallness of the room, not only sang but danced in a way that reminded me of Tevya in *Fiddler on the Roof*. We sang a final prayer before the icons on the porch and made our way home by tram.

Kiev, April 22:

Boris isn't impressed with the practice in churches in the west of receiving communion with very little or no special preparation. "In the Orthodox Church we ask people to receive communion at least four times a year and we ask them to prepare beforehand for at least two days. It has to be something special. We need to come to communion with a sense of awe, even fear, fear of God. We say to people in the liturgy, 'With fear of God, and belief, draw near.' In preparation we don't only want people to fast but to pray frequently, pray on the tram, pray while waiting in lines. We ask people to come to morning or evening prayer in the church."

We tried to see the Mother Superior at the Pokrovskye Convent but she was away. I did manage a brief conversation with Sr. Elykonida, who has been there thirty-seven years, is a member of the choir, and a reader in church. I asked how the convent had changed since she joined the community. "Hardly any change at all! We are living and praying now and we were living and praying then."

And that was that. Yet she said in a few words what is and was and always will be at the centre of monastic life.

"She is a real monk," said Boris. "She doesn't like lime-light. She doesn't want to give a speech and it is no honour to be interviewed by a journalist. And she hadn't been blessed by her superior to talk with you. But perhaps you would have done better with her if you hadn't said hello. Never say hello or good morning during Easter. In Easter season, Easter is every day, not only Easter Sunday. You have to say, 'Christ is risen!' "

In the afternoon Boris, Lydia, Volodya and I went to the movies to see *Pokayaniye* ("Repentance"). Last February, in

131

Moscow, I tried to get a ticket to see the film. It was showing in seventeen cinemas around the city but tickets were completely sold out. It was easier to see the Bolshoi Ballet. Tickets were unavailable in Leningrad as well — Boris and I went to the opera. But here Boris finally succeeded in getting tickets. Even then there were only a few vacant seats in the theatre despite the early hour and the fact that it was a weekday. "It's said that Gorbachev ordered enough copies of the film to be made so that everyone will see it," Volodya told me. If the rumour is true, Gorbachev must be pleased.

The film, directed by Tengiz Abuladze, was made in 1984 in Georgia, the Soviet Republic where Stalin was born. It ended up on ice with all but a few prints destroyed. That even one print survived is credited mainly to Eduard Shevardnadze, who backed Abuladze in making the movie. At the time Shevardnadze was First Secretary of the Communist Party in Georgia. Now he is Foreign Minister of the USSR and one of those most identified with Gorbachev. Following Gorbachev's election and the subsequent overthrow of the Brezhnev-era old guard in the film-makers' union, the film was finally released.

Ostensibly about the mayor of a Georgian city, *Repentance* is really about Stalin. The dictator is a parable-like figure named Varlam who not only resembles Stalin but Hitler, Mussolini and Napoleon. Varlam is one of those people who, even after death, have a continuing awful presence among the living, becoming objects of veneration to those who are dazzled by cruelty and raw power. Their death is a kind of nap. In one scene we see Varlam/Stalin waking up in a lidless coffin, grinning dangerously at the camera, then rolling over to make himself more comfortable.

After Varlam's burial his body, black boots and all, keeps re-appearing, propped up in the garden of the family villa. Death seems unable to contain this man responsible for the deaths of millions. The family, who thought they had seen the last of the Great Man, become increasingly distressed and call in the police to put an end to all these undesirable resurrections. A night watch in the cemetery reveals that there is nothing magical about

Varlam's post-mortem mobility. The daughter of two of his victims has been digging up the corpse and is using it to haunt Varlam's slick, modern, high-living descendants.

The story centres on the parents of the grave-digger. We meet them earlier in their lives, when their daughter was eight or nine. They are a young couple, both artists. In our first glimpse of the couple their faces are lined with apprehension as they watch Varlam give a speech from a balcony facing their home. On a gallows in the background a vulture sits complacently on the cross beam. In the sky, Varlam's portrait is suspended from a balloon. (In fact there were similar pictures of Stalin decorating the Soviet sky fifty years ago.)

The man has a Christ-like face, the woman looks like Mary and wears a cross. In a prophetic dream the woman sees herself and her husband buried in the earth. Only their faces are uncovered, their eyes open and alive.

The couple are trying to save a local church that has been turned into a scientific laboratory — Boris guessed it was meant to represent the huge Saviour Cathedral that once stood across the Moscow River from the Kremlin, now the site of an outdoor swimming pool. The camera slowly explores the peeling frescoes of biblical scenes before it discovers the shining apparatus of high technology that has taken the place of worshippers.

Varlam, flowers in hand, visits the artists' home and seeks to win their support with an excess of charisma. In fact Stalin occasionally sent flowers to those whom he had added to his death list. Varlam pretends sympathy with their desire to save old buildings, but after his departure, the church is burned and the two artists — first the husband, then the wife — are swallowed up in the gulag. We see the man again when he is dying under torture. As the camera closes in on his suffering face, one realizes that it is also the face of Christ dying on the cross.

There is a heart-rending scene of his wife, warned that she is about to be arrested, trying to escape with her daughter in the dead of night, but grabbed as she steps out the door of their dingy flat.

133

The couple's daughter survives. By the time of Varlam's death, she is devoted to baking cakes modelled as churches, each steeple crowned with a golden baptismal cross such as her mother wore. One of Varlam's admirers in the film is a curiously stunted man wearing an old soldiers' uniform who, paying more attention to the newspaper than to what he is doing, takes the steeple from one of her edible churches and, cross and all, stuffs it in his mouth. His eyes are held by the headline announcing Varlam's death.

The film's images have the brilliant clarity of dreams. In one scene people are waiting in line at a prison gate to deliver letters to relatives. If a letter is accepted, relief floods the face of the person who brought it. But for many the voice behind the gate refuses the letter, saying only, "Left, no forwarding address." Those who wait know the awful meaning of the words. This is no film-maker's visualization of nightmares but simply how it was.

In another scene several women are in a muddy timber yard searching the ends of the logs. One fortunate woman finds her husband's name and, weeping, caresses the rough wood as if it were her husband's face. Over supper I asked Boris if this was a dream scene. "It was no dream," Boris said. "It was common for people to search among logs for names. Prisoners working in the forests carved their names and dates as a sign that, at least until the date on the log, they were still alive. What you saw happened many times."

Repentance spans three generations. So little of the terrible truth has reached the third generation that Varlam's privileged grandson has no idea of the horrors that are buried in the family past. His discovery of them leads him to accuse his father, a powerful man living elegantly in his mansion. "You don't understand," the father angrily tells the son, "you don't know how it was! We did our best!" The boy barricades himself in his room and shoots himself.

His death drives the father to repentance. He goes into the cellar of the house where paintings that had belonged to the murdered young artists are stored. The room is now a kind of chapel illumined by vigil candles. In this setting the paintings resemble icons. Varlam's son gazes at himself in a cracked mirror and watches his own image dissolve into the face of Varlam leering at him, laughing satanically. The image fades. In the darkness near the mirror a half-visible figure silently raises a fish to his shadowed face — the face of Christ — and eats it. In the darkness, in repentance, there is eucharist and forgiveness.

More than anything else, this is a religious film. In the final scene we see an old lady asking the woman who makes church-like cakes, "Does this street go to the church?" "No, it is Varlam Street — a street named after Varlam can't lead to a church." "What good," asks the old lady, "is a street that doesn't lead you to a church?" The film ends as we watch this babushka hobbling down the barren street.

Repentance is destined to be seen in many countries but only in the Soviet Union can one see not only the film but the stunned faces of the audience as it files silently out of the theatre.

After supper we went to a local church, the Parish of the Ascension. We were too late for evening prayer but in time for a meal with the pastor, the church warden and his wife and several guests. In a snug room painted pale green we enjoyed a meal of potatoes, fish and wine, plus two bottles of Russian champagne.

We talked a little about the possible ordination of women to the priesthood. The warden's wife, Larisa, who keeps the parish accounts, was very animated, with bird-like quickness of movement and eagerness in speaking. She was wearing a dark red dress with a bright blue kerchief over her black hair. She said she would be willing to have women ordained if the church were in a situation of there not being enough men. "Until then the woman is called to be a mother, that is her first duty, and we should do that if there is no need to be priests. As it is now, there are four or five men for every place in the seminary so there is no necessity."

"She is right! She is right!" a couple of other women replied. "But within the house, she is the priest," another woman said firmly. "Yes, that's true," one of the men responded, rather ruefully I thought. "But we should at least have women deacons. This was done in the early church." About this there seemed to be agreement. I sat next to Bishop Basil, visiting from Washington, who for so many years couldn't get a visa. "Times really have changed," he said.

From Larisa I learned something about parish finances. Each parish gives ten per cent of its income to the diocese. Another ten per cent goes to the Soviet Peace Fund. In this small parish, ten per cent equals 20,000 rubles — a lot of money. Larisa counts the money, pays out what is due to the diocese and the Peace Fund, pays the parish bills, and pays those employed by the church — the priest, the deacon, the reader, a few of the singers in the choir (most are volunteers, but for a few this is their vocation or at least part of it). "I also pay the taxes," she says, "and that's a lot of money, almost half for a priest, because legally he is self-employed and therefore in the highest tax category."

At the end, we faced the icon corner and sang the final blessing.

Kiev, April 23:

We met with the abbess of the Pokrovskye Convent, Igumenya (equivalent to Mother Superior) Margareta. In the convent she is referred to simply as *Matushka*. She was busy with convent matters when we arrived. Another sister brought us to a large room with several desks. On the wall we found photos taken in the 1880s when the convent was founded. It looks much the same today. Other pictures were of the Russian Orthodox monastery at Mt. Athos in Greece. We noticed several photos of Kiev at the turn of the century including a photo of the monument by the Dnieper commemorating the baptism of Russia in which we could see the cross that originally was on top. The room was full of plants. Though it was a chilly day, the room was full of light and felt almost tropical.

Matushka Margareta came in. She was wearing an ordinary black habit and a black fur cap. Her face is faintly lined. She sat at her desk turned toward us, very still, steady, attentive. Under the glass covering her desk were postcards of flowers, churches, birds. Occasionally she rested her hands on an abacus. (The abacus is still in wide use. Wherever buying and selling go on in Russia, no sound is more familiar than the clicking of abacus beads.) She had a rosary in her hand.

I asked about daily life in the convent. "We get up at 4 or 4.30 and at 5 we have our first prayers. Then at 8 there is the Holy Liturgy, a public service. Because of the nature of certain jobs, not every sister can be at the Liturgy, but in some cases jobs can be rotated so, as much as possible, each sister can participate. At 11 we have breakfast and then each person has some jobs to do — gardening, care of the sick, cooking, cleaning, making bread for the church, receiving guests. We have many guests! Lunch is at 3 and then more work until the Evening Service, also public, at 5. The church is open until 8 or 9. There is a service of compline just for the community at 10, and then we sleep.''

How about accepting new members? How do people enter? ''First, those who wish to come prepare themselves before coming. They think about which monastery and which Rule they should follow. When they apply, they are interviewed. We ask them why they want to come here. Generally they say, 'I would like to serve and pray and for me the monastery is the most suitable life for Salvation.' After that they have time to visit, to look, to try it, to see how we live, what we are doing. It is one thing to know by words and speeches, another to live the life. Then, if we see she is a suitable person, we admit her to the community.''

How long is the novitiate? ''There is no standard time. It depends on the person. If she is well prepared, she might be allowed to take the vow quite soon. Before this happens, we discuss the person in the Council and we make a decision together. If we agree, then we ask the Metropolitan to give his blessing. Only then does the sister put on the habit. For some it can be a long time before that happens. People are different, different by age, experience and by Spirituality. In any event we expect people to be forty before they take the first vow and we do not accept people into the community before they are thirty. When a sister is at least sixty, if she is a good one, if she is eager to do more, then she may be allowed to take a second vow, the *schema*. In that case she has no other duty except to pray. She goes to all the services, and really she is praying all the time, for herself, for the community, for the church, for the world. We have twenty sisters who have taken the second vow.''

I asked if she could tell me more about the prayer life. ''We pray the Psalms all day, the sisters doing this in turns of one hour. As long as we have been living here, there has been constant prayer. Every day we receive requests for prayer for particular people, both living and dead, and this becomes a part of our life of prayer. We pray the rosary. This is an essential part of the spiritual life of nuns and monks. We wear it around our wrists when not using it. To read a book, you need light. Perhaps it will bother someone else. But to pray the rosary, you need no light and you disturb no one. In our tradition, we don't need to repeat the same prayer all the time but can say ten of one, ten of another, 'Lord, have mercy on me,' or any prayer or sentence from the Bible that is helpful.''

I asked about Easter. ''Easter is not Easter without Great Lent. As believing people, people believing in the Resurrection of Jesus Christ, we need to prepare spiritually and so need to keep Great Lent. We need compassion and communion. We need to take part in church services and to pray wherever we are. We need to deepen our feeling for others. We need to discover repentance. During Holy Week, we need to think and feel why we are here in this world, and to consider that Jesus was crucified for us, and that we too need to take up our cross and follow him. We believe that Jesus was raised from the dead, and that all of us will be raised as well, so Great Lent is preparation also for our own resurrection.''

''Preparation for Easter can't be expressed in words — one has to *feel* it. It isn't just certain things we don't do or don't eat. We don't eat anything made from milk or eggs. We in the convent never eat meat, and during Lent we don't eat fish — but these things are only the surface of Lent. What we are mainly doing is spiritual celebration. We have a song: 'We are fasting not only by flesh but by soul.' ''

Has religious life changed in the Russian Church over the centuries? ''We know that a lot of believers are doing much in a spiritual way, but it is also clear that we are much weaker nowadays than those who went before us. We have to try to be more as they were.''

What about the educational level of sisters? ''Some of us are well educated, but not me. I speak just as an ordinary person. I grew up in an ordinary Christian family. But all we really need to know is that life doesn't need fine words. You have to live it. You have to offer a good spiritual example to others — not just words but how you are living. This isn't only for monks but for every Christian person. But we who are living this life, we have a special responsibility. God asks more of us."

Before parting she let me take her picture. I asked her to pray especially for my family and told her something of my own family history. She had Boris write the names in Russian. Then and there we turned toward the icon in the corner of the room and where she prayed for each person named "that the light of faith would shine in their life." She said she would continue this prayer regularly. At the entrance to the building Boris took a picture of us together and then she watched us drive away.

After lunch and a visit to the Ukrainian Art Museum, Volodya and I went book browsing. We had noticed a set of Shakespeare in a particular shop but it turned out to the Ukrainian translation. We enjoyed the search and had a good look at the centre of Kiev.

Volodya often refers to the stories of Somerset Maugham. "I remember almost all of Maugham's stories. Of course he was not a genius, but very talented." Sometimes he asks if a certain person we have met doesn't remind me of a particular character in one of Maugham's stories. Matushka Margareta reminded him of someone in the story, "Painted Veil."

The longer we are together, the more often Volodya recites poetry, sometimes in Russian, sometimes English. Today, inspired by a painting of a peasant woman's face that we had seen in the museum this morning, it was one of Shakespeare's sonnets:

Shall I compare thee to a summer's day?
Thou art more lovely and more temperate . . .

After a "good-bye-to-Kiev meal", we hurried to the station to catch the night train to Odessa but it turned out we had read the ticket wrong. We thought it was leaving at 9.55 but it was *train* 55 and it left at 9.31. We arrived at 9.35, just in time to see the train disappearing. For the next hour I guarded our suitcases and read Gorky while Volodya got the tickets validated for a refund and Boris made a futile effort to see

140

if there might be an alternative way to get to Odessa that night either by train or plane. We took the tram back into the city and in the morning caught a flight to Odessa.

Odessa, April 24:

Boris, Volodya and I are staying in an old, rambling guest house of the Ascension Monastery on a high embankment above the Black Sea a few miles west of Odessa. We have also acquired a babushka, Sr. Invof, who is short, slightly cross-eyed, dressed in faded black, wearing a stained cotton apron. Her name, Invof, means love. She has been at the guest house thirty years but belongs to a nearby community, the Convent of the Nativity of the Mother of God, where there are about sixty nuns. She has a look of bewilderment on her face whenever I say anything in Russian. When I asked her if I could take her photo, she turned toward the wall, hid her face in her apron, and wouldn't turn around until I promised not to point my camera toward her.

The Odessa Theological Seminary is fifty yards away. Next door is the summer home of the Patriarch of Moscow. An orchard stands between the guest house and the sea: pear trees, apple, plum, cherry. The paths run under grape arbors.

We arrived at the monastery as people were streaming out of the main gate. The morning service was over, bells were ringing and, at a well near the church, one of the monks was distributing holy water. Everyone was carrying at least one bottle, jug or pail of water.

On the flight from Kiev, reading a book borrowed from Boris' library, I became engaged in an essay by Alexander Schmemann on "Worship in the Secular Age" which happened to include a section on water:

> To bless water, making it "holy water", may have two entirely different meanings. It may mean, on the one hand, the transformation of something *profane*, and thus religiously void or neutral, into something *sacred*, in which case the main religious meaning of "holy water" is precisely that it is no longer "mere"

water, and is in fact opposed to it — as the sacred is to the profane. Here the act of blessing reveals nothing about water, and thus about matter in the world, but on the contrary makes them irrelevant to the new function of water as "holy water". . . .

On the other hand, the same act of blessing may mean the revelation of the true "nature" and "destiny" of water, and thus of the world — it may be the epiphany and the fulfillment of their "sacramentality". By being restored through the blessing to its proper function, the "holy water" is revealed as the true, full, adequate water, and matter becomes again a means of communion with and knowledge of God.

Now anyone acquainted with the content and the text of the great prayer of blessing of water, at Baptism and Epiphany, knows without doubt that they belong to the second of these two meanings, that their term of reference is not the dichotomy of the sacred and the profane, but the "sacramental" potentiality of creation in its totality. . . [9]

The same essay defines secularism as "a negation of worship . . . the negation of man as a worshipping being, as *homo adorens*: the one for whom worship is the essential act . . . It is the rejection of the words, 'It is meet and right to sing to thee, to bless thee, to praise thee, to give thanks to thee, and to worship thee in every place of thy dominion . . .' "

Fr. Schmemann recalls a twelfth century Latin theologian, Berengarius of Tours, who argued that, because Christ is mystically and symbolically present in the Eucharist, he therefore isn't really present. The Lateran Council condemned Berengarius, declaring that, as Christ's presence in the eucharist is real, his presence is not mystical. Schmemann sees such border-drawing between the real and the mystical as the foundation of secularism. It is the loss of a sense of unity between the visible and invisible, a quality essential to authentic Christianity. "It was the collapse of the fundamental Christian understanding of creation in terms of its . . . *sacramentality*." Ever since, he argues, western

9. Alexander Schmemann, "Worship in the Secular Age," in *For the Life of the World: Sacraments and Orthodoxy* (Crestwood, NY: St. Vladimir's Seminary Press, 1973), pp. 131-32.

Christianity has embraced dualism, breaking existence into the realms of supernatural and natural, the sacred and the profane. Schmemann fears such dualism is gaining ground in Orthodoxy.

How the Russian Orthodox are coping with secularism, I can't say, except it is clear that nothing is more central to the lives of believers than prayer, and it is apparent they have a profound sense of the sacred that intimately concerns such ordinary things as bread, wine, salt and water.

I asked Boris how the holy water received today will be used. "People will drink a little of it after their morning prayers, and if someone is sick they will give them some, or put it on the part of the body that needs healing."

Not everyone had left the monastery grounds. People were sitting together on benches and on the grass eating bread and Easter eggs and visiting together. Some had their meals in the cemetery. In America we don't picnic around grave stones.

Our host is Fr. Inocenti Shestipol, one of the forty-four members of the monastic community and teacher of church history at the seminary. He has a round face, red beard, clear, pale blue eyes, and looks at me intently whenever he speaks. He gave us a tour of the grounds, then took us into the seminary where we saw lecture rooms, auditorium, residence rooms, library, reading rooms, infirmary, and administrative offices. It's an impressive establishment. Though nearly one hundred and fifty years old, the seminary has been here only seventeen years, having moved from the central part of Odessa in order to be linked with the monastery. In the same period student enrolment has doubled. Now they have two hundred and forty-five students. Four to six beds are jammed into the residence rooms. Next to each bed, or on the adjacent window ledge, I noticed students had made personal Easter arrangements using Easter egg, flowers, pussy willows.

We met with the rector of the seminary, Fr. Alexander Kravchenko. His hair is like a lion's mane, but grey. He has been active in ecumenical dialogue, and especially mentioned Cardinal Willebrands, head of the Vatican's Secretariat for Christian Unity.

"Though our seminary is very traditional," he said, "at

the same time we aren't standing still. Life pushes on. It is a dynamic age, and we have the ecumenical movement, which brings to the seminary theologians and pastors from every section of the Christian church, and also Jews and people from other religious traditions. This kind of encounter never happened a generation or two ago. It isn't always easy. There are many things we don't agree about. Yet we learn a great deal and sometimes there are surprising points of connection. Also we have had conversations here with Old Believers [from the schism that happened within the Russian Orthodox Church four hundred years ago]. We take them in our arms! From time to time we receive people active in the peace movement, especially the part of it that is within the churches. Recently there was a meeting here with the Pax Christi movement. So we are not living inside a shell.''

We looked together at a collection of photographs of Odessa, which included some awful pictures of what happened in the last world war. ''Too often in this world people display their weapons,'' Fr. Alexander said. ''It is better to show our faith and to hold hands, to gather together, to do together whatever we can to keep safe the gift that God gave us. I know people have said this to you before. You hear it again and again in our country. For 781 days Odessa was occupied, and before that we experienced the Civil War, so it is inevitable that we are preoccupied with peace. We always try to show people the cost of war, even the old kind of war that happened here. And now we face weapons that would make the world fit only for cockroaches!''

As a parting gift, he gave me a medal of the Apostle Andrew. ''We believe that Andrew was near here, perhaps even stood at this place, before he went up the Dnieper River. We keep his feast on December 13th in a special way. We pray he will help us continue to make new the Church.''

We drove into the city in a shining 1956 black Zil with faded blue curtains and plush upholstery. It was Russia's answer to the American fishtail Cadillac. Despite its years it is still a royal barge.

Odessa is a park-like city of wide avenues and nineteenth

century buildings mainly done in the classical style though with touches of *art nouveau*. Houses are soft yellow, orange and dark red. Those with two or three storeys often have wrought-iron balconies. Though it is still cool here, the city has a southern temperament. There are trees everywhere. The harbour is crowded with ships. Odessa is a huge port, second only to Leningrad in the Soviet Union. Perhaps Odessa's most striking sight is the wide stairway, the Potemkin Stairs, that links the seaport to the tree-lined Primorsky Boulevard in the upper city. Before returning to the monastery for the night, we stopped at the memorial for the war dead, left flowers and prayed.

Odessa, April 25:

We spent several hours this morning in the catacombs east of Odessa, limestone quarries that have served as a place of hiding in times of war and revolution. During the last world war the catacombs were the main base for the local resistance. When we turned off our flashlights, we could begin to imagine how much resolve was needed to make one's home in this damp, chilly, ebony world. It is definitely not a place for anyone with claustrophobia. At one point during the war, these winding passage ways had a population of four thousand. Kitchens, dormitories, meeting rooms, shower room, workshops, classrooms and hospitals can still be seen. The Germans walled up the entrances they could discover, tried repeatedly to smoke and gas the partisans out, but the passages run warren-like for a thousand miles. There were always undiscovered entrances. One was down the shaft of a village well.

Returning to sunlight from the underground world, we went on to the nearby village of Usatovo where the parish priest, Fr. Basil Prokofia, welcomed us. He is a short man, hobbit-like, with large, compassionate eyes and an immense grey beard. His church is one hundred and sixty-five years old, was recently re-painted in the old Russian style, and is dedicated to the Assumption of Mary.

As we stood in the middle of the church, he told us what had happened in the village on Palm Sunday, April 9, 1944. "The Soviet troops were getting close. Because the fascists were losing, they wanted to punish the local people. At the end of the Holy Liturgy they came to this church and shot the priest and all the people praying here. After that they went into the houses in the village and killed everyone who didn't have time to hide in the catacombs. When they left, two hundred and seventy people in Usatovo were dead, many of them old people and children. Until today we remember each person who died. We keep them in our memory and pray for them by name. And we pray again and again for peace, never again to know such horrors. We pray, 'God save us, save us, keep us from war'. We pray to see a new heaven and a new earth. We ask any Americans coming here, when you go home, please tell your neighbours that we are peaceful people. We want to have friendship and to fulfill the prayer of our Saviour that we may all be one.''

His wife and daughter had prepared lunch for us in their home near the church. I admired the nut-stuffed prunes, a special Easter dish. That evening one of Fr. Basil's parishioners came to the monastery with a jar of these for me to take home to my family.

On the way back to Odessa, Fr. Inocenti talked about what Fr. Basil had said in the church. ''It must be difficult for you hearing so often about war. Each family has at least one person who was killed. For me it was my grandfather. But our experience is hard for Americans to believe or understand. What has happened to us makes us a little like survivors of a fire who say to a child, 'Please, never play with matches.' We have had an experience of war that most Americans, even many Europeans, have never known. And now we have had the experience of Chernobyl with consequences we still don't know. America is like a wealthy man. The wealthy don't know what it is like to be hungry.''

After supper Boris and I went for a walk through the orchard to a ledge overlooking the Black Sea in back of the Patriarch's summer residence. We sat on a sheltered bench that looks down on the beach and out on the water. After a time, a monk came by and sat with us. He and Boris talked in Russian, and I half-listened, half-watched the light on the sea, painfully aware that I don't know, can't know, what it is to be Russian, to live here, to remember what Russians remember, and to struggle in this particular society. But at least I can experience the faith of many of those I meet, and their strength and pride, and get occasional glimpses of anger, impatience, anxiety and grief.

We walked back to the guest house. Volodya had been out for the evening and returned with a friend, Alexi, and we sat in the darkness by the piano while Alexi played and sang melancholy ballads.

Odessa, Sunday, April 26:

There was a remarkable scene at breakfast. Sr. Invof, not as meek as she looks, exploded at the two young seminarians who wait on our table. There is a television in a corner of the dining room and she discovered them watching it. "Turn that off! You want to become monks, but here you are watching television while the Holy Liturgy is going on in the Church." They blushed, turned off the television, and bowed their heads to her.

The second Sunday of Easter resembles the Feast of All Souls, November 2nd, in the Catholic Church. It is a day of remembrance and prayer for the dead. As at the Easter vigil, families bring food — Easter bread, Easter eggs — to the church to be blessed. At the (Uspensky) Dormition Cathedral in Odessa, the lower church was filled throughout the day. Priests were blessing the food and praying by name, in Slavonic chant, for those who had died. Afterward families went out to the cemeteries. I saw them approaching one large cemetery in steady streams from several directions.

In the upper part of the Dormition Cathedral the Holy Liturgy was being celebrated. Orthodoxy brings to the Liturgy everything that is best and most beautiful — icons, silk vestments, candles, incense, and music. Every bridge of the senses is used to open the soul. The choral music today moved me to tears. It seemed simultaneously to rise out of the earth like a spring, and to fall from heaven through an opening in the sky. It is as soulful as black spirituals though the rhythms aren't the sort for hand-clapping. It is music that embraces the listener body and soul. I felt transported into timelessness, with a profound sense of God's presence not simply within the church but everywhere. "To sing," said one of the Church Fathers, "is to pray twice."

After the Liturgy, we went into the Church baptistery. In the centre of the large room was a basin on a stand for baptizing infants and, in the corner, a baptismal pool with steps going into it for adult use. On the other side of the room is a long table with dividing partitions with room for seven infants. Already young parents with their new-born children were waiting their turn. The priest who was our host said that three thousand children and to two hundred adults were baptized here last year. On the baptistery wall are quotations from the Church Fathers plus the texts of the Our Father and Creed. One of the texts read: ''Baptism is salvation and repentance and new life and white clothing and the way to heaven and the gift of being God's child.''

We went looking for the Fine Arts Museum and found the Pushkin Museum instead. In 1823-24, before going to Mikhailovskoye, Pushkin lived part of his internal exile in this building, then a hotel. In those days Odessa was a young dusty town with no paved streets, one small newspaper, four book shops and a population of twenty thousand. It was a far cry from sophisticated Leningrad. At least there was a theatre, and Pushkin never missed a play. He wrote many poems and the last one hundred and forty lines of *Eugene Onegin*. The woman who showed us around the museum is one of those guides who is doing exactly the right thing, introducing others to what she loves most. She has been there many years, but when she recites Pushkin's poems, you feel her joy is still fresh. ''Pushkin was,'' she said with pride, ''the first Russian exiled for poetry.''

We stopped to watch children playing on the streets. There had been storms in the small hours of the night, but by the afternoon the sky had cleared. It was warm and there was the first hint of summer.

Back at the monastery guest house for a lunch of meat-filled pancakes, we were joined by the Dean of the Cathedral, Fr. Simeon Kravchenko, and a younger priest, Fr. Victor Petluchenko, who lived in Canada for several years and speaks English with ease. He teaches comparative religion at the seminary.

I asked Fr. Victor to say something about himself. "Well," he replied, "first of all, I am a good man! Now you know it and so you won't have to take a long time to find out."

We talked about the significance of the day's outpouring of people to all the cemeteries. "We are still mourning people who died forty-five years ago in the war," said Fr. Simeon. "We remember them and we still cry. We also remember what it was to be hungry and to live in ruins."

When I remarked how good the food was, Fr. Simeon laughed. "Not long ago we had one man who was in a delegation from Great Britain who brought a suitcase of bread and canned food. His wife told him that he was going to a land where no one smiles and people are starving. Instead he found that too many of us are over-eating and that it is not only for religious reasons that some of us need to fast! In the end he decided to take the food back because otherwise his wife might not believe that we are have not been hungry for many years and that we even laugh."

I was asked about my impression of the morning's church service and said how moved I was by the music. "I'm relieved to hear it," said Fr. Simeon. "The main thing we seem to hear from western visitors is that we are just a church of old women. It's a way of saying we don't matter, that we are dying out. If you look closely, in fact you see every kind of person at the Liturgy, but I wish visitors might have the chance to know one or two of those old women they seem to wish weren't so numerous in our churches. The old women, the babushkas, are still the majority. They are the great force in our church. Though it is seventy years since the Revolution, we have a permanent supply of grannies! And these are the most determined people when it comes to prayer. We have quite a long service in our churches, especially in Lent. You would think these old ladies would be grateful if we found some ways to shorten the services, left out some minor things here and there. But if a priest dares to do that, the next day we will have complaints about it at the Metropolitan's office from these same old women. They want to pray the same way their grandmother and grandfather prayed. They can't imagine another way. That is our immortal granny. Don't look down at her. Look up to her.''

Fr. Victor commented, ''Old or young, sacraments are our life. It isn't as sometimes people in the West say, that we are just stubborn and don't want to move an inch. For us the short services in the Western churches are like city air that you can't really breathe in. We like a liturgy that is country air. To celebrate the sacraments takes time but it means clean air, and we can't get used to less than that.''

After lunch, Boris, Volodya and I went back into the centre of Odessa. At the Church of St. Elijah, prayer for the dead was going on. Easter Bread, Easter eggs and candles were on the table set up for the day's special services. The priest singing the prayers looked exhausted and sounded hoarse. It gave me a glimpse of the hard labour it is to be a priest: two services every day, baptisms, weddings, funerals, confessions, a lot of things to do and often a crowd.

We saw an exceptionally beautiful icon of Mary and Jesus in this church — her long hand touching his tiny face. Mary's hand, so big and sheltering, was itself a ''protecting veil.''

Fr. Victor stressed that the working churches in no way depend on government help. ''What you see in our churches we did ourselves. You see that iconostasis? One woman spent a year repainting it and applying the gilt. And the gilded wood carving around this icon, this was done by a man in the congregation.''

We had an hour in the Fine Arts Museum. A painting made in 1906 by Gabriel Gorelov caught my eye. ''It shows the removal of church bells in the winter of 1700,'' said Fr. Victor. ''A quarter of Russia's bells were melted down to make cannons. The tall man in the foreground with the moustache and the determined expression is Peter the Great. Ignoring the protest of prelates and believers, he used the bells to make cannons. Those cannons were a factor in the Russian victory over Sweden which gave us access to the Baltic Sea and led to the founding of St. Petersburg.''

We found a painting by Sergei Ivanov, done in 1910, of a European walking through a Moscow crowd in the sixteenth century. The Russians, in colourful robes, were laughing at the European, a slim man in severe black and white looking every inch a figure of purpose and profit. "Westerners were called *nemtsy,*" Fr. Victor said. "It means people who are mute. As far as clothing went, it was men like him who had the last laugh. Peter the Great ordered the men to cut their beards and both men and women to dress like the westerners, though such clothing is not so practical in Russian winter."

Back at the monastery, I talked with Fr. Victor about Catholicism. He venerates Pope John XXIII. "We Orthodox," he said, "couldn't stand the First Vatican Council [1869–70, a Council that centralized church administration and proclaimed the dogma of papal infallibility]. When John became Pope, we knew the age of the Inquisition was over, that the Catholic Church no longer regarded itself as the 'one true Church' but rather as a Church among Churches. Responding to Pope John's invitation, we sent Metropolitan Nikodim of Leningrad as an observer to the Second Vatican Council and we have a better view of that event. But I have some troubles with the present Pope, John Paul II. Perhaps because he comes from the Polish Church, where there was such an intense struggle between eastern and western forms of Christianity, he seems to favour a rebirth of the Uniates [churches that retain some features of the Byzantine Liturgy but are in communion with Rome and whose bishops are appointed by the Pope]."

We talked about similarities and differences between Orthodoxy and Catholicism. "Russian Orthodoxy is less institutional. We are not quite as attentive to discipline and give more stress to mercy and forgiveness. I think it is fair to say that we have understood Christianity less as a system of doctrines and more as a way of life. Lay people have a bigger role in the life of the Russian church — our church is less clerical. We have a unique category of sanctity, the 'passion bearer,' the person, like Sts. Boris and Gleb, who refuses to defend his life even though he has the right to do so. We pray on our feet and we pray at length. The Catholic church is musical, but we are even more musical! But the similarities are many and deep. We both have the sacraments and apostolic succession. These are the corner-stones of both Churches."

He asked about my wife's name. "Nancy would be Anastasia," he said, "and that means Resurrection. So you are married to Easter. And you are Dmitri — the Apostle James!" We said our goodbye.

"Until we see each other again," Fr. Victor told me, "please, no sinning!"

Odessa, Monday, April 27:

After saying thank you to Sr. Invof, we drove in our magnificent Zim to the airport. On the way Fr. Inocenti expressed the hope that my book would help heal the wounds that many Russian refugees suffer in their exile. "A lot of Russians who fled after the revolution are still missing what existed here before. They are very bitter. But my view is that what happened was somehow God's will. It does no good to be angry, to hate, to be bitter. We need to look at what is good. When we prepare for communion, we need to put aside all hatred."

Before leaving Odessa, I discovered that the residents of the monastery are not only monks. There is also at least one family of foxes. I discovered a fox hole behind a hedge. It was big, deep, and well-established, evidence that the monks have made room for a patch of the Peaceable Kingdom. I was reminded of a painting by Nesterov in which a bright red fox, in a posture of submission, is approaching a young monk.

At the airport I said goodbye to Boris. Today he returns to Kiev. From the air we had a final glimpse of the Black Sea. Odessa was shining in sunlight, laced with green avenues and looking like a city on the Mediterranean.

Moscow, April 27, continued:

It was two degrees above freezing when we arrived. The sky was a mass of thick grey clouds. We were met by a theological student and were driven directly to the Danilov Monastery where Metropolitan Filaret of Minsk, head of the Department for External Church Affairs, was expecting me.

The Metropolitan is a former rector of the Seminary at Zagorsk. Born in 1935, his father was a famous professor of music, his mother a teacher. Both were devout believers. On the walls of his large panelled office are various icons and the symbol of the World Council of Churches. There were intricately painted Easter eggs on his desk. He was wearing a grey cassock.

He spoke of the need for Orthodox parishes in new residential districts. "We are by far the biggest Church in this country," he said, "but not the fastest growing. The Pentecostal churches and other sects are growing more rapidly. Part of the problem is that it is complicated and slow founding a new Orthodox parish. It isn't only a problem from the state side but the slow way we do things in our Church. But if new Orthodox churches aren't opening, then the spiritual energy existing in each person pours into other churches and take new forms. From our point of view it is a sad development as our conviction is that only the Orthodox Church can correctly form religious outlook and practice. The meaning of the Russian word for Orthodox — *Pravoslavie* — is 'the right way to give glory.' "

We talked about the crisis in relations now going on between the Greek Orthodox Church and the government in Greece, where the state will no longer tolerate the Church having so much land and control of property. "We see once again," said the Metropolitan, "as we have said to the bishops in

Greece, that what we fail to do ourselves others will make us do. This is a lesson we have had to learn with much pain."

He referred to a group of Americans he had met a few days before: "It still surprises many visitors to see how vital the churches are here. Many people still do not expect to find a living church in the Soviet Union. They think opposition can destroy a church. In the United States I often have the sense that believers are without a positive understanding of suffering. But attacks are not so terrible for the Christian! Christians suffered before. We are ordered to suffer. But the Saviour is with us, he is with the whole world, and he will give his peace to the whole world."

A problem for American visitors trying to understand the Russian Orthodox Church, I said, is that in the United States we explain everything, while Russian Orthodoxy expresses itself through imagery, music and liturgy. "It's true," he said. "We tend to try to conceal our spiritual life. When you try to put what is deepest in life into words, you find there are no words. What you want to say is clear, but there are no words. This is the reason our church is not famous for books of theology."

Asked about my family, I remarked on the impact of Russian Orthodoxy in our home life. "Your wife is part of what you are doing, just as the wife of a priest shares in the priesthood. Your wife is a *matushka* and she should come with you to Russia. You haven't yet seen my part of Russia, White Russia, the real Russia. I am inviting you and Nancy. It isn't just a polite word. I ask you and Nancy to come this summer. You will be my guests." He gave me a final blessing and an Easter egg to bring home to Nancy.

Volodya's sister, Ludmilla, had made an Easter supper for us at their small apartment (actually the apartment of their parents presently serving a parish in Tokyo) on the north edge of Moscow. Besides Easter eggs and Easter bread, Ludmilla had prepared *pasha*, a pyramid-shaped Easter treat made of cream cheese, butter, egg yolks, sugar and cognac. We ate sliced salmon and beef roasted with garlic and drank strawberry wine and champagne. On the wall and mantel were many icons. Volodya played a recording of Easter music sung at the Holy Trinity Lavra. I spent a long time browsing through their bookshelves, which include Ludmilla's collection of English dictionaries.

A friend, Anatoli, dropped by. I asked him what is it that draws young people into churches. He responded, "I explain it my way. Our world has an amazing system of life, but it's seldom that people think about it — the meaning of time, the meaning of day and night, the way the world is, the stars, the flowers, the people. Somebody wanted us to become a fact, with eyes, ears, legs. Somebody must have created all this. It didn't just happen by accident. This kind of thinking leads you toward God and thinking about God leads you toward the Church. Life has a meaning, a purpose. We are in this world to find where we belong in the next world. Life isn't just to eat and drink and go to the toilet."

We talked about films. "I have a friend who has been to many international film festivals," Anatoli said. "He finds that Russian films in general are better — more sincere, more noble and idealistic. I have this impression when I go to see western films in theatres here. I don't understand why these qualities are missing in so many films that come from the west. I know there are exceptions like *One Flew Over the Cuckoo's Nest*. But you don't seem to have anything like *Repentance*, a film that has a significance that cuts across all political and national lines and that has a deep religious meaning."

He asked, "Why do people in the United States like films with so much violence?" Volodya's response was more interesting than mine. "People in the United States," he said, "get their emotions from films. But for me real emotion is hearing the Hymn of the Cherubim during the Holy Liturgy. This is the peak of my emotions." Before leaving, Ludmilla gave me the recipe for *pasha* and invited me to return next time with Nancy.

JULY 1987

Before leaving Moscow in April, Metropolitan Fileret had invited Nancy and me to come in the summer to see "White Russia, the real Russia." Having found friends ready to take care of our children, we went to Moscow, a two-day train ride from Holland.

Brest-Moscow, July 18:

A Soviet border guard woke us at 2.30 a.m. We presented our passports and visas and made a customs declaration. The train entered a huge building in the railyard of Brest, just inside Russia's border with Poland. Every car was un-coupled and, passengers still inside, jacked up about three yards over a work pit. The old sets of wheels were then removed and wider gauge sets installed, a fascinating ceremony that took about an hour. We pulled into the Brest station, already bustling with people, as dawn was breaking.

All through the trip, the train picked up new cars, dropped off others, became re-linked in all sorts of ways. We began in Amersfoort as the only Soviet car on a train in which most of the cars were going to Copenhagen and Stockholm. By the time we crossed the Russian border we were part of a long assembly of Soviet cars all heading for Moscow.

We ate lunch in a Russian dining car added to the train at Brest: potatoes and beef stroganoff, more elegantly named than made. We seemed to be the only foreigners in the dining car. The women were hefty, with gold teeth, gingham shifts, quick, hearty laughs; the men were solid, plainly dressed, rolling cigarettes, enjoying themselves.

From the window we watched the summer scenery: attractive villages of wood houses, fields, gardens, children, people walking together, farms, animals. It was very serene. There was an old fat man with a cap, dress shirt, dress trousers and suspenders, sitting alone under a tree, a small meal beside him set out on a napkin. Factory-fresh orange and yellow automobiles were lined up at a train-crossing. Women were threshing wheat, kerchiefs on their heads, their children playing nearby in brightly coloured sweaters. There were women sunbathing along the tracks. Between villages there were pine woods, birch trees, heather, wild flowers. Getting close to Moscow, we passed through Borodino, where the great battle with Napoleon was fought that Tolstoy describes so vividly in *War and Peace*.

We arrived in Moscow at 6.30 p.m., four hours behind schedule, and were met by Vasili Maknev. He is huge, blond and was wearing red, white and blue braces. He tucked several suitcases easily under his arms, found a taxi, and took us to the Ukraina Hotel.

Moscow, Sunday, July 19:

We went to the Holy Liturgy this morning at a Moscow church near the Kosmos Hotel. We walked up the church steps past a group of elderly beggars and we dropped coins in their outstretched hands as they gave us their blessings. Nancy asked Vasili why there were beggars on the steps of the church when everyone is able to get food and housing in the USSR. "Some prefer to live this way," he said. "In fact it is an honour to be a church beggar. Each beggar must be accepted by the church and the congregation first." (Living in western Europe gives some perspective on this that one wouldn't have in America. In Holland, where everyone is entitled to housing and food, there are still some who prefer to live by their wits and close to the pavement rather than become objects of official care.)

Nancy wore a scarf and looked at home in a Russian church. We stood in the midst of old babushkas standing solidly on the floor, crossing themselves, bowing, and occasionally going down on their knees, touching their heads to the floor. In front of us a young mother stood with her little daughter of five or six. The child was quiet and still, and occasionally knelt down to relax. An old nun in black tried to make the girl more comfortable by offering her a small chair, but the girl preferred her mother's skirts. The nun stood in the front and received candles from people in the congregation who passed them up through the crowd. She lit them and set them in the candle stand.

Binding everything together in the Liturgy is a powerful sense of attentiveness. "Be attentive!" is a key phrase. (Vasili told us afterward that he sometimes leaves the Liturgy to walk outside, because he has foot problems and cannot always maintain his attention.)

A young priest with a rich deep voice and stylish haircut sang much of the service. When it came time for a sermon, an older priest came out to speak. These were the only spoken words in the whole service. All the people drew up close to hear his sermon about Jesus' healing and forgiving.

"Our Lord," he said, "before he healed the body, forgave the sins. Repentance is at the root of healing. As sins are forgiven, as we become well spiritually, our body is also affected. Everything is connected. Sometimes our awareness of being sinners makes us ill. So Our Lord says to us, first of all, 'Go and sin no more.' This is the lesson of today's Gospel. Listen to these words and try to grasp their profound meaning. We are called to accept the love of God. If we do that, we will be both happier and healthier. May Our Lord heal us from sins and disobedience and lead us to his kingdom."

Nancy wrote in her journal: "I have never been in a congregation of such unqualified religious concentration. I had a sudden sense of being at the centre of the universe and knew that each of us had this in common. The fact of standing rather than sitting may have something to do with remaining attentive to the activity in the church rather than slipping into private daydreams or plans for the rest of the day. You can't help but pay attention to the sensuous drama going on, the brilliant iconostasis, the constant singing, the incense. All these things pulled me again and again to the business at hand, the eternal present, with its music. I had such a deep sense of spiritual connection."

After the Liturgy we walked in the cemetery behind the church. In a tree-shaded, weedy place against a wall we found signs of someone's encampment, a sleeping mat and old clothing neatly arranged on the ground. "It could be the grave-diggers," said Vasili, "or a mad person, or even a Fool For Christ's Sake, someone who lives on alms with no permanent home, who gives advice and counsel to people. In Russia a Fool For Christ's Sake is revered in a special way."

He recalled such a woman back in Leningrad in the last century, Xenia, who camped out near a chapel. Many people came to her for advice. When she died, people still came to the place where she had camped to reverence her. The people in the church finally roped off the area and preserved it. She is regarded as a saint though she not formally canonized.

"Russia has always had a tradition of pilgrims and holy fools and wise sages," said Vasili, "and this tradition continues even today. I have the name of one of the most famous of them, Vasili or Basil. He lived in Moscow in the time of Ivan the Terrible, wore almost nothing, walked barefoot on snow and ice in the winter, and had the courage to accuse the czar. He was like John the Baptist. Amazingly the czar left Basil alone. Perhaps he even feared him. When Basil died, he was buried next to the cathedral, officially named the Cathedral of the Intercession of the Mother of God. Because the Muscovites regarded him as a saint, a chapel was built over Basil's grave and became part of the church. So the church built at the order of Ivan the Terrible has taken the name of one of the few people in Russia who wasn't afraid of the czar."

After lunch we went for a long walk, first to a museum devoted to Pushkin, then through a residential district near Arbat Street where Vasili grew up, then on to Red Square.

On Red Square I marvelled once again at St. Basil's Cathedral, so playful, so *un*-serious, like a huge page from a children's book. "But the paint they used on the last paint job was too cheap," Vasili complained. "It was painted only a few years ago — now it needs to be painted again."

Our walk took us past half a dozen book shops along the way, all closed because it is Sunday. "Russians are readers but we don't have enough paper," said Vasili. "The result of the shortage is that, among authors, the living fight the dead. Second-rate books by living authors are printed in huge editions while the works of Dostoevsky, Tolstoy, and Pushkin are always in short supply."

Nancy found it strange to be in a city without advertising. "In the States, everybody wants to sell," said Vasili. "Here, everybody wants to buy." Vasili lives in a two-room apartment that costs twenty rubles a month. "That means it is

166

almost free," he said. "You can use your money for other things, but perhaps not what you really want. There are all sorts of shortages, and no one ever knows why. There are plenty of supplies, plenty of labour, yet even in Moscow we have a shortage of workers. Or at least we have a shortage of workers who work with real care. Perhaps you heard the story about a foreigner visiting a factory. 'How many people work here?' the guest asked the factory director. 'Oh, about half,' the director answered."

Moscow, July 20, Monday:

I asked Vasili how it happened that, in the early sixties when so many churches were closed, one church remained open for worship, another shut its doors. "Each church has its own story. There is one church that I know which was ordered closed yet stayed open just because the wife of the chairman of the local Council of Religious Affairs made holy hell for her husband until he agreed to let the church stay open. A famous scientist, a rocket designer, lived near the church you went to yesterday. There are statues of him and his face is on postage stamps. He was a believer and worshipped at that church. He stood out of sight from the congregation, behind the iconostasis. Perhaps his being there was all that was needed to protect that church."

Nancy asked about religious discussion groups in Moscow. "Moscow is full of sects, bursting with them," said Vasili. "We have people talking about astrology, several schools of Buddhism, different kinds of meditation, every sort of Christianity, a lot of Bible study groups. People are starving for anything that might give meaning to life and sometimes they make strange choices to fill the hole. But in the Russian Orthodox Church we discourage discussion groups. There is the old Russian saying, 'Opinion is the mother of all suffering. Opinion is the second Fall.' You can form study groups only with the blessing of the Church and with some appropriate person to give guidance so that people don't wander off on their own track. Otherwise people get lost in their opinions, everyone reading the Bible in his own way, always finding exactly what he wants to find and missing everything else. You end up with Christianity in a thousand little sections and everyone hating each other. The theologians are permitted to have their own theological opinions, but not the rest of us.

It isn't our tradition. We pray together and believe together. For Orthodox believers the main place to hear the Bible is in church. The Bible was written for reading in church as part of worship, not for discussion clubs.''

The Holy Trinity-St. Sergius Lavra, Zagorsk, July 21:

Each time I come to Zagorsk I am caught by surprise. Zagorsk, for all its ancient buildings, is always a place of the present moment.

The most memorable part of this visit was the time we had with a young monk named Father Alexi. He spoke to us chiefly about the vital importance of mystical union with God through Christ: that it is possible, that it is worth one's total efforts, one's life, that indeed life is empty and pointless without it, and that it only happens within the community of faith, the Church.

"This Lavra is the centre of the Russian Orthodox Church, and St. Sergius is the heart of the Lavra," Fr. Alexi said in welcoming us. "His heart encompasses the whole world."

As we stood before a model of the Roman catacombs where Christians worshipped during times of persecution, Fr. Alexi asked, "What caused this obedience to Christ? What caused believers to risk their lives but never to threaten anyone and never to defend themselves? The Christians could have taken up arms but instead they gave up their lives. They had the strength of obedience to Christ. Obedience is of the utmost importance, even obedience to death. They gave witness — the Greek word for witness is martyr — with their own blood."

As we stood before the oldest icon in the seminary collection, dating from the ninth century, he said: "Icons also are witnesses to Christ. It has been said that the fact that there is a Holy Trinity icon painted by Rublev is proof of the existence of God. Without communion with God, such an icon cannot be made. Without God we are not capable of such beauty. A lesser beauty has its roots in a greater beauty.

"Culture is based on cult. Culture forms us. In the Russian icon, the Russian recognizes his own culture, his self, because it is the Russian vision of God, something absolute. It comes from union with God. Western art is a big step down from this. It mirrors the culture only as an image of people removed from union with God. The state of the soul is reflected in what one paints and what one wants to look at.

"God teaches us how to get in contact with each other and how to treat the world. A useful way to understand our relationship to God and to each other is to picture God as the centre of a wheel with ourselves at various points on the radii. As we approach God, the centre, we approach each other, and as we move away from the centre, we move away from each other. You cannot approach God without approaching others also. God asks us to love our enemies. That's difficult! But it is the way of perfection. We are called to achieve it. Someone isn't a saint because of his high morality but because of his communion with God. It is out of that communion with God that a saint loves his enemy. He cannot do otherwise. Love of enemies can occur only with love of God. The two happen simultaneously.

"Christ didn't say *thinking* is the way. He said love is the way. But sometimes it looks like madness. You have heard about the Holy Fools, the Fools for Christ. Some of the saints intentionally put on the mask of madness. Under their rags they often wear a heavy metal cross. Without a purified heart this wouldn't be possible. It is done to achieve the gift of humility without which it is impossible to love anyone.

"It is said that one of the Fools for Christ was taken into heaven where he saw many saints but not the Mother of God. He asked the angel guiding him where she was. 'She is on the sinful earth helping humanity.' He realized that the saints can enjoy all the gifts of paradise but they continue to be with us in our suffering.

"There are seven hundred basic models of icons, and far more models of sanctity. But in each case the perfected Christian has not achieved perfection through his own good works, but by faith, which can come only through the sacraments, only through the Church. We cannot be saved alone. We must be part of a community."

He pointed to a fifteenth century icon of St. George slaying the dragon. "The dragon represents evil. But it isn't St. George who slays the dragon. If you look at his hand, you see he isn't really holding the spear, just touching it lightly. This is to show that it is only the strength of God that overcomes evil, not our own strength."

St. Paul, in a nearby icon, is shown holding the Bible with a powerful grip. "You see him full of life, ready to sacrifice himself. You feel his anguished love of his brothers and sisters so profound that he was prepared to be separated from Christ if that would draw others closer. The Bible is shown in reverse perspective. The Bible is smaller for the person standing in front of the icon than it is for St. Paul. You realize that you are only at the beginning of the road of faith. It is only in deeds for God's sake that we start on the way to God."

We stood before the relics of St. Sergius: two chalices made of wood, several small icons, one of his sandals, a tool he used in making wooden toys. (Zagorsk is still renowned for its wooden toys.) Fr. Alexi said that there are still experiences at the Lavra of people encountering St. Sergius. "In one case a pilgrim came from a remote part of the country and had made no arrangements to stay anywhere for the night. It began to rain. An old man came up to him and asked, 'Why are you standing in the rain? Please join me.' They walked for fifteen minutes to a little cabin. The old man gave his guest bread and water and a bench to lay on. When the man woke in the morning, the cabin was gone. The pilgrim discovered he was under a fir tree. He told the monks what had happened. They knew that once again St. Sergius himself had cared for another pilgrim."

We eagerly listened to everything Fr. Alexi said, like hungry people being fed. We could sense his excitement and the mounting enthusiasm he felt as he shared more and more with us. Finally, when we parted, he thanked us for our attentiveness, and said, "I think one day you will become naturalized Russian citizens."

172

Fr. Alexi spoke so intently and with such clear devotion and intelligence that even Vasili was impressed, "old hard-boiled egg though I am."

Moscow, July 22:

Waiting for the Kremlin gates to open this morning, we discovered a group of Americans among the crowd of Russians. An elderly American woman asked a young Russian couple if she could photograph their little girl, about eight years old, who had big white organdy bows in her hair ("a fifty-year-old hairstyle," said Vasili). "I have a granddaughter of my own," the American told the Russian couple in a heavy southern accent. The Russians didn't speak English but understood her desire, and proudly adjusted the little girl's hair bows. The crowd cleared a space, the girl stood very still, looking serious and nervous. Her parents looked proud. The American woman took the photo and thanked them all profusely. The gates opened and we went on for an unhurried visit to some of the oldest parts of the Kremlin.

In the afternoon, we went to the Danilov Monastery, still being prepared for the millennium. The air was filled with noise and dust. We saw a group of workers gathered around a cross and singing a litany for the dead over the grave where bones unearthed during the restoration work were being re-buried.

We were received by Metropolitan Fileret who told us about a group from the American National Council of Churches who were currently in the USSR to prepare to serve as guides for groups of American Christians who will take part in the millennium. "The guides, all of them Americans, met with Patriarch Pimen in Zagorsk yesterday," he said, "and sang for him a Psalm in Church Slavonic! I never expected to hear American Christians singing in our language. And they were good."

He mentioned that Protestant visitors are sometimes disturbed by all the imagery and icons in the spirituality of

174

Orthodoxy. "But actually everyone has some icons, though perhaps it is a photograph of someone they admire or whose music they especially like. The photo of the earth from space is a contemporary icon, an icon for both believers and unbelievers."

We spent the evening with Volodya and Ludmilla at their apartment, one of several identical, huge blocks. We took a rather shaky lift up to their floor, the fourteenth, where Volodya met us. Ludmilla has been reading *The Habit of Being*, a collection of the letters of the American writer, Flannery O'Conner.

Moscow, 23 July:

Visiting the Novodivichy Cemetery today, we stopped at the grave of Gogol, whose stories I had been reading on the train from Holland. "He was, if I may say, a nuisance to himself," said Vasili. "He was thin, shy, very nervous, yet was deeply loved by everyone who came in close contact with him. He wrote some of the best, funniest stories in the Russian language. Some people say he saw visions. At the end of his life he wrote a letter calling on his friends to turn to the Holy Orthodox Faith. This brought him a lot of criticism. People said he was crazy. For a Russian it is funny to think of him being translated into another language. We can't imagine it."

After lunch we went to the State Council for Religious Affairs where we met with Yuri Smirnov and Sergei Kuznetsov. The Council is widely regarded as being the state's instrument for keeping believers on a leash. There is a tradition of such structures in Russia since the time of Peter the Great. I went expecting a formal and perhaps grim encounter. In fact it was a lively meeting that opened with a discussion of the recent visit of Cardinal Sin from the Philippines. "The Cardinal was amazed and deeply moved at the vitality of the churches in Russia," Yuri Smirnov told us. We had already heard similar accounts from others. "But Cardinal Sin's willingness to come to the Soviet Union remains exceptional. Some Catholic bishops were invited to the Peace Forum, but none came. Catholics seem to be the least willing to accept invitations to visit our country. We especially hope that more American Catholic leaders can come here. If the Orthodox Church invites them, the door is open and our Council will do whatever we can to help them see whomever they want to see and go wherever they want."

We also talked about religious rights in the USSR. "In the

past there were many instances where the rights of believers were not respected. But this is changing. In this Council, we see our function as assuring that the rights of believers are respected, not denied, and we try to be a bridge between religious bodies and state institutions when believers have needs, for example when they need use of state-owned building equipment for restoration of churches or construction of new ones. New legislation is now being drafted which we expect will much improve the situation of believers in this country. This involves consultation with all religious groups. We hope the legislation will be ready by next summer, in time for the millennium.''

Moscow, 25 July:

Today, with Vasili away, we went on our own to see the inside of St. Basil's on Red Square. We arrived early while the queue was short, paid our few kopeks and then wandered through the narrow passageways decorated with vine-like geometric designs. Under each dome is a small chapel. In the lower church we discovered a large icon of a Fool for Christ's Sake, emaciated and wearing a loincloth while listening attentively to divine messages from above. It was St. Basil himself.

Ludmilla had invited us for lunch. We took the Metro and bus to get there. It was a beautiful afternoon. We bought a big sack of tomatoes for a house gift from a street vendor at the bus stop, and walked across a muddy, weedy lot until we found the right building. Ludmilla was in her apartment with a friend who seemed to understand English but did not speak it. We ate bread, tomatoes and cucumbers, sausage, and drank *kvas*. We talked all afternoon, and exchanged stories about living in New York, about her parents, her religious experiences, and about icons.

Ludmilla told us an icon story: "I had been so ill that everyone was worried that I would die. I fell asleep in my illness, and had a dream in which I was walking on railroad tracks that extended infinitely into the dark. Down the tracks, a woman came walking toward me, dressed in black, with white hands and bare white feet. The woman said to me, 'Don't worry, the train isn't going to hit you.' When I woke up, I was well. I wanted to get right out of bed, but my mother insisted that I not get up so soon. I told my mother about the dream, and she said, 'That was the Mother of God.' The next Sunday, I went to church. One nun who had been praying for my recovery said she had a gift for me — an icon of the Mother of God. When she gave it to me I immediately recognized the face. It was the same face that had been in my dream." Ludmilla showed us the icon. It hangs over her bed.

On a crowded bus going home, an old man getting off whispered something in my ear. I was at a loss as to what the man had said and then it hit me. It was an international whisper between men: "Your fly is open."

We ate supper and went to the station to catch the train to Smolensk. Over tea in our compartment, we talked about Solzhenitsyn's novel, *The First Circle*, set it prison in Stalin's time. "It is a courageous subject but it's not a book I admire," said Vasili. "The prisoners don't sound like prisoners, they sound like graduate students. The book's main problem is that it doesn't reveal that prison is boring, a piece of life stretched into eternity."

Smolensk, Sunday, July 26:

Smolensk, "the key and gate of Russia," is the most western of ancient Russian cities. On the north end of the River Dnieper, it is at the source of the water highway that leads past Kiev to the Black Sea.

Father Victor, a quiet young priest, met us when the train pulled into the station at dawn. After checking into the hotel and having a brief rest, we went to Holy Liturgy at the Cathedral of the Dormition, the principal Smolensk landmark, a five-domed green and white building standing at the top of a steep hill in the centre of the city. Inside the cathedral is a mammoth, heavily gilded iconostasis from the eighteenth century that includes not only icons but statues. There is also a baroque pulpit, not an element of Russian church architecture until the time of Peter the Great.

Archbishop Kyrill was presiding, a man in his forties, among the youngest bishops of the Russian Orthodox Church. He has a greying black beard and a clear, direct manner. For ten years before coming to Smolensk he was rector of the Leningrad Theological Academy where he is credited with many of the innovations that happened there, including the introduction of women students.

While he stood in the centre of the church with his arms outstretched, attendants vested him. It as though he were no longer himself, but a moving, praying, singing part of the liturgy, all connected with the church, the icons, the music, the incense, the Eucharist.

The church was crowded. There were the usual deeply pious old women, among them one woman on her knees at the front rail, eyes fixed on an icon, crossing herself and bowing over and over again. Russian tourists moved in and out, watching rather than participating. Despite the almost continuous motion among the people and the clergy, and the constant music from the choirs, there was a powerful sense of attentiveness and stillness.

No one hushed the children in the church. They obviously enjoyed being there. We noticed a priest and his family in a vacant choir stall. One daughter looked to be twelve and her little sister about four. The older sister was holding the little one up on the rail and they were hugging and stroking each other. All the while, the older girl joined in singing the words to all the prayers and hymns.

The day's Gospel was the story of Jesus healing two blind men. A sermon followed by Archbishop Kyrill. As he began to speak, the congregation gathered around him, standing with their hands relaxed at their sides, completely attentive.

"Our Saviour said to the blind men, 'Do you believe I can heal you?' They said, 'Yes, Lord.'[1] And then he healed their blindness.

"This story makes me wonder about wonders. A wonder is something that surprises. It goes past the border of usual experience. We see wonders and we call them miracles. But there are people who reject the possibility of miracles or anything that goes beyond their own experiences. They say, 'It cannot be.'

"What the Church teaches is that wonders are special expressions of the love and power of God. When we experience or contemplate wonders, they inspire wonder in us.

"St. Augustine says that the normal growing of wheat is akin to the multiplication of loaves. So much of the beauty of the natural world awakens wonder: sky, sun, plants, water. 'Look at these things,' says St. Augustine, 'and see that they are beautiful. Their beauty is their confession of God.'

"Most wonders stand on laws that are the foundation of the world, in which everything is developed. And isn't this too a wonder? When God does things beyond our understanding, even then he is acting within the laws of the universe.

"Not to see beauty, not to be aware of wonders — this is to be blind and deaf. The French scientist Pasteur said that

1. Matthew 9:27-31.

181

the more we contemplate the world, the more we are filled with wonder.

"Some people can see wonders, some not. Why? What makes it possible to become aware of the actions of God in the world? Do we need special education? Some special wisdom? No, dear brothers and sisters, the Gospel shows us otherwise. Christ said to the two blind men, 'Do you believe I can heal you?' Only when they confess that they do believe does he heal them.

"They were healed, but there were even at that time people who were not moved to wonder by what he did. There were those who said, 'Jesus casts out devils only because he is the prince of devils.'[2] What he does, they said, isn't a miracle. It is magic. And so they dismissed what Jesus did.

"Faith is the condition of wonder, not the other way around. Perhaps here at this moment there could be a miracle. Even then there would be people present who would leave saying, 'Yes, there was something strange, something we need to clarify.' In fact we find in the press stories about events for which there seems to be no natural explanation. But this doesn't mean people reading these stories are led to faith. Miracles don't give birth to faith. Perhaps that is why Our Lord in this Gospel forbids people to publicize what he did for the blind men. The news would add nothing to people's faith. It was not with wonders but with his words that he tried to soften people's hearts. A heart filled with love and faith can distinguish good and evil. The believer can cross any boundary with God.

"Love is the power of God. May God help all believers to be attentive to the wonders that, because of God's love, fill the whole universe."

The congregation replied, "God save you!"

While the Liturgy was going on, Vasili left us for about a half hour. When he returned he said that another priest had been giving a talk in the back of the church on such topics as the reception of communion, marriage and mutual help.

At communion, the children came first — all the children,

2. Matthew 9:34.

beginning with babies, held in the arms of their parents or other adult friends. The first in line was the twelve-year-old girl, holding up her little sister to receive the Eucharist. Communion is administered with a spoon while an attendant holds a napkin under the chin of the person receiving.

After the Liturgy, we were given a historical tour of the church by Fr. Victor. As we moved through the church, a crowd gathered around us just to hear what Fr. Victor was saying, straining to catch every word.

After lunch, we saw some of the city. Though Smolensk is more than eleven centuries old, very little of the ancient city has survived. Close to Russia's frontier and on the main route to Moscow, it has often suffered the cruelties of war. We saw the city's kremlin wall, once so important to the defence of Russia that the czar, Boris Gudounov, prohibited all stone construction elsewhere in the country until Smolensk's defences were complete. The walls have been restored and strengthened many times. In 1812, during the French retreat, Napoleon's troops blew up six of the kremlin towers. By the end of World War II, only eight per cent of the buildings survived and ten per cent of the population.

We came upon an old veteran whose uniformed chest was covered with numerous war medals. He was marching down the middle of a broad, carless boulevard as if he were part of a parade, except there was no one else. "We say that he is wearing his iconostasis," Vasili remarked.

One often sees men and women wearing their war medals, though rarely with such pomp and circumstance. Every day in Russia, there are reminders of the last world war. For many Americans, absorption in that catastrophe appears almost neurotic, a pathetic entrapment in the past. Living in Holland, I find the attitude much less surprising. The last world war is still an open wound for many of the Dutch. One Dutch theologian we know, a man in his forties, said to me, "There has not been a day in my life when I haven't thought about that war." But the destruction was much less in Holland than here.

We went to a city war memorial erected on the site of Nazi

mass executions. The memorial consists of a grave mound —
a barrow — that was constructed by local citizens who each
contributed a handful of earth. There is also a statue of a
sorrowing mother evocative of Russian iconography. Near
the memorial is a big children's playground, filled with
laughter, a merciful reminder of the power of life over death.

We went to a little art museum that had some magnificent
icons and an ancient statue of King David that was simply
wonderful. The museum guide was excited, knowledgeable,
interested. We learned a great deal about the woman who
founded the collection, Maria Tenisheva. "She was a female
Tretyakov," said Vasili, referring to the founder of the
Tretyakov Gallery in Moscow.

We had a brief visit to a Museum of Linen, one of this
region's main industries. It seems that White Russia takes
its name from the white linen garments peasants wore in
ancient times. As the museum is a former monastery, we asked
Fr. Victor whether Smolensk wanted to have a monastery
again. "Not yet," he said. "You cannot have a monastery
with only four or five monks. Also we don't yet have a strong
enough infrastructure of active believers. People in this region
are not regular about attending church. Sometimes we only
have four hundred in the cathedral for a service. So we aren't
yet ready for a monastery. Monasteries are part of a deeply-
rooted community of faith. But we do have monks serving
in local churches and we have a number of pious women
dedicated to prayer and service."

Walking this evening in a park near our hotel, we came
upon a handsome statue of Pushkin. His face has strong,
negroid features. Pushkin's grandfather, Peter Abramovich
Hannibal, was an African who rose to national power and
became a noble under Peter the Great. Whatever criticism
one makes of Peter the Great, he wasn't a racist. The statue,
Vasili told us, is the work of a woman sculptor, a remarkable
postscript to his remark the other day about there being no
great women among Russia's artists, writers, and poets.

Vasili is such an astonishing fellow. He is vastly proud to
be Russian. He is a devout believer. He is a great reader and

lover of poetry. He has travelled widely. He relishes his work and is excellent at it, speaking English effortlessly and with feeling. He was Billy Graham's translator a few years ago, and told us how Graham insisted that Vasili not only translate the words but mimic Graham's gestures with the Bible. Vasili, a born dramatist, happily obliged. Vasili was Margaret Thatcher's translator this year during the Church part of her visit to the USSR. He became so engrossed in conversation with her at Zagorsk that she had to remind him to eat.

Vasili also loves things American — American kitsch, he says. In addition to his red-white-and-blue braces, he wears a Jefferson nickel tie clip reading "In God We Trust." When he can dress casually, he chooses a khaki short-sleeved Boy Scouts of America shirt. He knows more jokes than anyone I know, and the better we get to know each other, the funnier and more outrageous the jokes become. And he is a wholehearted male chauvinist. It says a lot that Nancy and he get on so well nonetheless. In fact it is a blessing to be with him. When we aren't serious we are laughing.

Smolensk, July 27:

After a morning of being rained on in the countryside, we visited Archbishop Kyrill. He lives in a small house with a view of the Dormition Cathedral. The dining room table was laid with candies, cookies, and a delicious cake. Coffee, tea and vodka were served.

I asked why so few adults had received communion at the Liturgy yesterday. "Yes, it is still very few, but more than used to come. Now it can be fifty on a Sunday when it used to be not more than five. Things change, but slowly. Before the Revolution, it was common for people to receive communion only twice a year. People were overwhelmed by their sense of unworthiness. Patriarch Pimen has made a call to believers to receive communion as often as possible and this appeal is being heard. But with this there has to be a process of religious education. We try to offer that in the church and actually prefer doing it there. We would rather not have something like that happen in a school classroom. Part of the process of religious education in our diocese is to have a priest on duty throughout the day in the cathedral where they can answer questions. We find that if one person asks a question, immediately others gather and you have a group discussion."

Archbishop Kyrill is a member of the Executive Committee of the World Council of Churches. "I got into the ecumenical movement as a 'youth.' It was the sixties, a decade when everyone was bowing their heads to the young people. The experiences that opened to me through the World Council of Churches have made me realize that the ecumenical movement and work for the renewal of humanity and peace are profoundly linked to each other. What enthusiasm there was for Christian unity sixty years ago! Not that I was there, but what a spirit of youth, power, and passion there is in papers presented at early ecumenical conferences. They are filled with both joy and pain, with longing for unity and sorrow for division."

Nancy commented on how much more vital churches are in the Soviet Union than in Holland. "The problem in the west is not organized atheism but secularism and the consumer psychology. But we may face the same thing in a few years, so we watch anxiously what the church does in the west as this may help us. But perhaps we also have something to offer the church in the west, some encouragement, some lessons. It is important to know something of the church that exists in the first socialist state."

I asked about the tendency for more young people to become active believers. "Certainly there is an encouraging influx of young people right now but we have to be careful not to limit our perception of who is a believer by only noticing who is standing in the church. The process of coming to belief is very complex. We are aware that many people are believers in their world outlook even though they rarely go to church. The tip of the iceberg are the people you see in church, and that tip creates the image. These are people permanently in church, often retired people, mainly elderly women. But the iceberg is one object, not two, even though most of it cannot be seen. Also that babushka that looks older than the world — in fact she is younger than the Revolution. She never attended a church school. She memorized no catechism. As a young woman she never went into a church. But sometime in her life she became part of the visible church. There is always a large group of believers who are struggling with this decision, and slowly, as they become older, they begin attending church. The invisible part of the church is much younger, but today they more quickly become part of the visible church. They aren't waiting for retirement. The democratic events going on in our country help this process. We see more and more people coming who never came before, never showed any sign of belief. Now they want to belong to the church. It seems like a fresh development, something completely new, but actually it has deep roots.

187

"Yesterday you saw quite a lot of people in the church you might say were just tourists. I don't think more than twenty per cent of the people were crossing themselves. Many of the women weren't wearing scarfs. But a lot of those who seem to be just watching are on the border of belief. They don't stand there for two hours just because it is a beautiful old building. Something draws them. They are not practicing believers, but they are there. And who can say who is a believer and who is not? We don't know that. Nobody knows."

We said good-bye and hurried to catch the train to Minsk.

Minsk, July 27:

We arrived at 10.30 p.m., and were met by Fr. John, a middle-aged priest with a goatee, very gentle and proper-looking, who brought us to the Intourist Hotel. It was almost midnight when we ate supper. The dining room had a live rock band producing music so loud that we could only talk during the breaks. At one point, the band sang, in English, "The Final Countdown."

Minsk, July 28:

We ate breakfast early with Fr. Leonid, a middle-aged, animated man. Afterward a tour guide drove us all over the city giving us a monotonous drill of important sights with many dates, measurements and numbers. Vasili translated in a sing-song voice. At one point we passed a new "micro-city" in the north of Minsk. "It has everything a person needs," said the guide, "shops, cinemas, clinics, day-care centres, schools, athletic facilities." "Does it have a church?" I asked. The guide was lost for words, then said with obvious embarrassment that this was something local people have to work out with the state. Vasili, suppressing laughter, barely managed to translate the reply.

Under all the statistics the guide heaped on us was the fact that Minsk, though nearly a thousand years old, was so flattened during the last world war that afterwards there was serious discussion about moving the entire city to a new location and starting on fresh foundations. In the end it was decided, however, to build at the same turn in the River Svisloch. Except for a few old buildings that have been restored, Minsk today looks thirty years old.

No one place in Russia brought home to me so starkly the horror of war as our visit in the late morning to Khatyn, about thirty-five miles north of Minsk. Khatyn today is a memorial commemorating Nazi atrocities in White Russia. Hitler's plan had been to take White Russia, kill 75 per cent of the population, and bring the rest to Germany to do forced labour. In fact 2,230,000 people were killed, one White Russian in four. The Germans used a scorched-earth policy, simply levelling villages and slaughtering the inhabitants. Hundreds of villages were totally destroyed, many never re-built.

Khatyn, one of the erased villages, is a shrine to all who

perished. In the case of Khatyn, the German soldiers appeared one morning, herded the villagers into a barn and burned them alive. Those who ran out of the flames were shot down with machine guns placed around the barn. Then all the houses were destroyed. Two children survived and one man, Joseph Komensky, a blacksmith who happened to be out of the village at the time. Returning home, he found the dead body of his eleven-year-old son in the barn. A huge statue depicts him with his dead child in his arms.

The foundation of each house is outlined in concrete. Each contains a chimney with a single leaden bell. The bells are timed to ring once every thirty seconds, a dull death-knell tolling steadily as visitors walk through the village. There are burial stones for each village destroyed, and a long wall with barred windows, each window commemorating those who died in Nazi concentration camps that dotted White Russia. Visitors place fresh flowers daily at every stone and window.

There is finally a large flat square stone slab with three birch trees. Where the fourth tree would have been is an eternal flame. One out of four.

From Nancy's journal: "Though crowded with visitors, Khatyn is a hushed place. As we walked, I thought these people are not interested in fighting another war. They are ordinary, good people, they go on vacation, they care for their families, they love their country. Yet we in the west are preparing to do this very thing, to burn these innocent people alive in their own homes because we have labelled them communists and we think the world would be a better place without them. We are being lied to, I thought over and over again. The monstrosity of this fact pounded in my head. Lied to. Lied to."

Before we left, Nancy started to cry. Fr. Leonid rushed up to her, kissing her hand twice, and said, "Thank you, thank you!" Among those who died in the war were his sister and brother. He told us later of the disbelief he has experienced when describing to people in the west Russia's war experience. "But perhaps they will believe you."

Back in Minsk, we visited the Cathedral of the Holy Spirit,

being renovated for the Millennium. The interior was slung with scaffolding and draped with canvas. The place was filled with priests, workers, and worshippers. Actually, though the air was musty with plaster dust, it had a jolly atmosphere. Fr. Leonid said the people who are working on the church, although professionals, are also members of the church. We went downstairs to the baptistery where there are long couches to accommodate those waiting to have their children baptized. In Minsk the demand for baptism is high and constant. As we left, a group of people with two babies came down for baptism. "And this is Tuesday," said Fr. Leonid. "You should see Saturday and Sunday!"

We went to Metropolitan Fileret's residence, a new building with an open central courtyard. Several priests met us, among them white-bearded Bishop Constantine, former abbot of a nearby monastery, who is tall and thin and venerable-looking.

Tomorrow we drive to Brest, stopping on the way at the Monastery of the Dormition at Zhirovitsy.

Minsk, July 29:

After an early breakfast, we went with Fathers Leonid and John to the Diocesan Residence to pick up Bishop Constantine, then stopped off at the Cathedral. We got a glimpse of about 30 people at morning Liturgy at a temporary location in a hallway, with candles and make-shift iconostasis. The plasterers were hard at work as the singing continued.

On the way out of Minsk we visited the Alexander Nevsky Church and met its dean, Father Victor Bekarevitch, an older man of incredible spirit and enthusiasm wearing a white cassock and gold cross. He told us all about his family, his children, grandchildren and great-grandchildren, how many sons and sons-in-law are priests, and the history of his church and the story of the saint it is named after, even a story about a particular church in Siberia. He was unstoppable, like a bottle of champagne that had popped its cork and was showering everyone. "Yes," he said, "I am a real talker. But you have to understand that this is only because I was baptized in boiling water! I can't help my temperament." He patted the top of his head.

We talked about living in big families. "They are best! One child is nothing. Two is only half a family. Three is a little better. But six is a collective farm! We have six."

When he heard I was a writer, he warned me to be careful. "It might be better to be a robber. The robber does his harm once and it is over. But writers continue to live on in their work and can destroy long after they die. I bless you to be a writer, only please write things that take care of life and inspire people to have many children."

On the way out of Minsk, all the Russians in our van prayed for a safe journey. It was joyous and hearty singing that reminded me of the soulful singing of Orthodox Jews at the Wailing Wall in Jerusalem.

Most of the way we were on a four-lane highway driving through pine and birch forest. After some time, we stopped to stretch our legs. Bishop Constantine got out and crossed the highway to walk through the forest on the other side. The rest of us wandered through the pines and birches on our side. Nancy and I went our own way, enjoying the smell of the woods and the feel of leaves and soft earth under our feet. We felt we had a little taste of what it might be like to go mushrooming, a favourite summer pastime in Russia. After about a quarter hour, returning to our van, we looked across the highway and saw Bishop Constantine crossing the four lanes of busy traffic, holding his white linen cap on his head, his long white beard and black robes flying. He barely escaped a big tractor trailer whose driver was leaning on his horn. "That was not a warning," said Vasili. "It was a greeting." We got in the mini-bus and sped down the highway, soon passing the tractor trailer. Sure enough, when we passed, the driver honked again, leaning out of his window and waving at Bishop Constantine with a big smile and shouts of greeting.

"My heart sings whenever I approach the monastery," said Fr. Leonid as we neared the village of Zhirovitsy. "It is my second motherland. It is even my first motherland. You should see it on the great feast days! Thousands come, pilgrims from far away."

The Monastery of the Dormition, the home of about forty nuns and fifteen monks, is surrounded by sweet-smelling orchards, gardens, and bee-hives. Several monks were busy in the garden. Two industrious nuns were scrubbing pickle barrels. The Abbot, Archimandrite Stephen, another possessor of laughing eyes and a brightly lit-up face, pointed out a family of storks in a huge nest up in a nearby tree.

The Abbot took us to the principal church where he told us the story of the miraculous icon that is displayed there. "On May 20, 1470, some children taking care of cows were playing near a pear tree. It was where the main altar now stands. There was a stream flowing from the tree and light coming from the water. The children approached the light and found a tiny icon of the Mother of God and her child. They took it to the landowner who put the icon in a box. That night he decided to show the icon to his house guests. But when he opened the box it was gone. The next day the children found it again in the same way. This time the landowner took the icon to the bishop. A wooden church was built over the site where the icon appeared, but fifty years later, a terrible fire destroyed the forest, the church and everything inside. Everyone sadly realized that the icon was also gone. A short time later, however, village children discovered a beautiful lady — it was Mary — sitting on a large rock. She had the icon in her hands and gave it to the children. The children ran to fetch a priest. Soon after another church was erected over the site of Mary's appearance. That stone became an altar.'' The icon's fame reached Rome. In 1730, the Pope awarded a crown to the icon. The tiny icon is here, an object of veneration to pilgrims every day.

After pausing under a huge tree near the church that had been planted by Peter the Great, we had a wonderful meal with the abbot: vegetarian borscht and vegetables wrapped in grape leaves. I asked the abbot about the life of his community. ''We are only instruments in the hands of the Mother of God,'' he said with a very joyful expression. ''She is our Mother Superior. Every morning, before the Holy Liturgy, we ask her blessing. We approach her icon and pray, 'Mother of God, help us!' The choir sings, 'Lord have mercy on us.' After the service the flame is carried from the icon to the kitchen to light the fire.''

I asked about all the pilgrims coming, which must impose a lot of work for the small community. ''There is a lot to do, but few *real* things to do. Our Lord finds people who are capable of fulfilling his plan. Maybe they have no education, perhaps nothing but their heart, yet God calls them to be pastors. I am such a person. I come from a peasant family. I came to the priesthood only through the faith of my mother.''

Leaving Bishop Constantine at the monastery, the rest of us continued on the way to Brest, a long ride, everyone but the driver napping on and off as we passed through the White Russian farmland. Sometimes it seemed we were in Iowa or Nebraska.

Brest, July 29:

We reached Brest as the sun was setting and went directly to the Cathedral of St. Simeon the Stylite, where we were met by three men belonging to the church council and two priests: Fr. Michael, whose smile revealed a number of gold teeth; and Fr. Arkady, a huge man, really bear-sized, but very quiet and with gentle eyes. One of the church council members had such a Polish face that he could have been the brother of Pope John Paul II. After a few minutes, a car came spinning into the church yard. Out stepped Fr. Eugene, Dean of the Cathedral, an older man with basset-hound eyes, a squarish goatee, and a head of wavy gray hair. He wears two crosses. He greeted us with emotion. Then Fr. Michael presented Nancy with a bouquet of roses and a bottle of perfume.

We went into the church as the choir began singing, a choir which just a few minutes before had been a group of babushkas and old men sitting outside under the trees in the church yard. The choir director, however, was a young man wearing tennis shoes and carrying a bulging brief case. Father Eugene greeted and blessed us, then surprised me by asking if I would say a few words. I said how wonderful it was to be received like Christ, as had happened to us daily through our travels in Russia.

We went to the Intourist Hotel afterward, accompanied by Fr. Eugene, Fr. Michael, Fr. Arkady, the three church council members and, still with us from Minsk, Fr. Leonid, Fr. John, and Fr. John's son, who had driven the van. It was a real parade with Fr. Eugene, in full priestly regalia, star of the show. Once in the hotel, Fr. Eugene negotiated with the women at the desk for our room and keys. He is a man of amazing charm and humour — many appreciative eyes were on him while we were in the lobby. The staff obviously enjoyed his teasing manner. Then the whole parade accompanied Nancy and me to our room, which turned out to be a small suite. Everyone checked the rooms carefully to make sure that all was in order. Fr. Eugene was unhappy with the two single beds separated by a night table. He removed the night table and two members of the parish council pushed the beds together. "That's better!" said Fr. Eugene. Having discovered that Nancy speaks some German, he said to her, *"Zusammen, zusammen!"* — together, together!

We went downstairs for a big meal with many toasts and much laughter. Fr. Eugene sat at the head of the table, placing Nancy at his right where he made sure that she participated in every toast.

A match for Vasili as a story teller, Fr. Eugene told us a joke about of a woman who was weeping bitterly at the funeral of her husband. "The priest came up and said, 'Don't cry so hard. Surely God will save him.' 'Father,' she said, 'you don't know why I am crying. It is only because he didn't die sooner. Then I could have married a good man!' ''

Vasili recalled a man for whom things weren't going well in life. " 'I want to get married but I have no possibilities,' said this poor man. 'I can buy a goat but I have no inclination.' Let us drink so that our possibilities coincide with our inclinations.''

After supper, we said good night to our crowd of hosts. Nancy and I decided to explore various streets and parks in the neighbourhood. On the way back we enjoyed watching a couple in front of us playing with their two little daughters.

At bedtime Nancy said she felt like she had been Queen for a Day. The meal had been like the wedding banquet we never had, with Fr. Eugene blessing us as Abraham must have blessed his children at their weddings. Being with Russian priests, she said, gave her a new understanding of patriarchy. "For me patriarchy has meant men running everything and the victimization of women. But to call a Russian priest a patriarch is to recognize him as an interpreter of reality, a person whom we trust to explain the truth of God." She said that from now on she will be sensitive to the difference between a patriarch who is spirit-filled and someone who is simply hungry for power and deaf to women.

Brest, July 30:

The parade — all eleven of us — reassembled for breakfast. Fr. Eugene asked, "And you had happy dreams, yes? *Zusammen?*"

He told us something of himself. He is forty years married and forty years a priest. As secretary to Metropolitan Fileret for the Brest District, one of twelve districts in the diocese, he has responsibility for sixty parishes. "It is a big responsibility, but my wife gives me strength. Her name is Nadeshda. It means hope. She rules my life."

I asked what he hoped to do in the future. "I like what I am doing. It is enough. I only hope not to become senile. I want to celebrate a last Holy Liturgy and then die, and it will be fine if this happens when I am two hundred and fifteen years old. By then perhaps we will be living in a world where you can knock on any door and borrow what you need and no one will need to lock their door."

We went out to Brest fortress, a huge war memorial. Here local partisans, with little food and water, held off the Nazis weeks after the rest of White Russia was occupied. It has been named a Hero Fortress, as many cities are Hero Cities — Brest, Minsk, Smolensk and Leningrad among them. Fr. Arkady gave us some flowers to lay at the eternal flame. We strolled up the long walkway with Fr. Eugene, casually talking. There were many tourist groups, all Russian. As we approached the flame, Fr. Eugene suddenly became silent and walked up the few steps as though he were approaching an altar. He laid down his flowers, as did we, crossed himself and prayed aloud. Guides had been addressing tourist groups standing nearby but they immediately stopped talking, turning toward the flame and standing in reverential stillness. When

Fr. Eugene's prayer was over, he bowed and crossed himself again and walked away. The tourist groups also left. It was as though Fr. Eugene had become the priest for everyone.

Across the stream from the Fortress are the ruins of a fourteenth century village. Archaeologists are still busy digging, looking for the ancient church.

We went home and rested. Luncheon, our last meal in White Russia, was long and cheerful. This time Nancy was seated at the head of the table, with Fr. Eugene at her right. Though we had only been in Brest overnight, we had become friends. It is remarkable how quickly you can feel kinship with people whose faith you share. He offered a toast in recognition of "the world-wide community of believers which knows no boundaries or national differences."

Soon Fr. Eugene was talking about holiness. "Holiness is what happens to people who open themselves up to God's love and to the power of the Holy Spirit. On your own you can only love a few people but with the Holy Spirit you can even love your enemies. You need to be guided by reason, but even more you need the guidance of the Holy Spirit. We are given freedom, but by ourselves we can use that freedom in terrible ways. We can do harmful things to ourselves and to others. I remember what William James said, 'If my faith were the faith of a woman washing underwear, it would have been greater than the essence of my mind.' Faith, life, community and family — all these are expressions of submission to the will of God. In God's will we can live in holiness. God grant that we live in God's will! God make us holy!"

All eleven of us went together to the train station and waited on the platform. Nancy and I sat on our luggage, watching people bustling all over the place — soldiers, parents with their children, old folks. When the train pulled in at 6.10, we found our compartment, carried in our luggage, and went outside again to say goodbye. Fr. John, who had been rather shy (certainly camera-shy) came up and, addressing Nancy in German, said, "We are so thankful that you came, and we wish you and your family the very best health. God bless you." Fr. Eugene gave us a solemn blessing and then hugged us in turn, making us promise one day to come back. "But next time," he said, "bring your children."

On the train back to Moscow, Vasili told us the story of an academician and a priest sharing the same compartment in a train. "The academician took out a bottle of yoghurt and two sandwiches and offered to share them with the priest. The priest opened his sack and took out salmon, caviar, roast chicken, sausages, vodka, and cognac. 'Here,' said the priest, 'take what you like.' The academician said, 'I am a member of the Academy of Sciences. I have a car, a chauffeur, a dacha, and I am paid 600 rubles a month, but I can't afford all that! How do you do it?' 'My dear son,' said the priest, 'you have to take more distance from the state!' "

Moscow, July 31:

After twelve hours on the train, we arrived in Moscow at 6.30 a.m. and went to the Ukraina Hotel. We had time for baths and writing postcards.

On the train I read an essay on icons by Vladimir Soloukhin, a contemporary Russian novelist and short-story writer: "I think that what the artist most often painted was prayer . . . a worshipper approaches an icon to pray and finds that his prayer is already expressed and translated into the painting. What is expressed on the panel exactly corresponds to the state of the worshipper's own soul. And in this exists not only the enigma but also the strength and persuasion of icon-painting, all of which escapes analysis if the icon be judged only with reference to line, subject and composition."[3] I read the passage to Vasili. He nodded and said, "I know a woman, a Party member, who was in a coma for a month. When she came out of the coma, her first words were, 'I want to paint an icon.' Today she is a believer."

On the wall of our room there is a fine oil painting from the 1950s that shows a bird's-eye view of the Russian countryside. In the distance, under a blue summer sky, is a village. Rising over the houses a white church tower blossoms into a dark blue cupola, but the cross that would top the cupola is missing. In the foreground of the painting is a pine forest. Two wide paths cut through the trees, intersecting at right angles. Looking at the painting, I realized that the cross that is missing from the church steeple has been cut into the woods. Once again, a Russian seems to be speaking through images rather than words. In this case he seems to be saying, yes,

3. Vladimir Soloukhin, *Searching for Icons in Russia* (New York: Harcourt, Brace, Jovanovich, 1972).

one can remove a religious symbol from a building, but no one can remove it from our hearts.

At five, Vasili takes us to the airport. It won't be easy to say goodbye.